How to Use Conversational Storytelling Interviews for Your Dissertation

How to Use Conversational Storytelling Interviews for Your Dissertation

David Boje

Aalborg University, Denmark and New Mexico State University, USA

Grace Ann Rosile

New Mexico State University, USA

Edward Elgar
PUBLISHING

Cheltenham, UK • Northampton, MA, USA

Published by
Edward Elgar Publishing Limited
The Lypiatts
15 Lansdown Road
Cheltenham
Glos GL50 2JA
UK

Edward Elgar Publishing, Inc.
William Pratt House
9 Dewey Court
Northampton
Massachusetts 01060
USA

Paperback edition 2021

A catalogue record for this book
is available from the British Library

Library of Congress Control Number: 2020942946

This book is available electronically in the **Elgar**online
Business subject collection
http://dx.doi.org/10.4337/9781839104183

ISBN 978 1 83910 417 6 (cased)
ISBN 978 1 83910 418 3 (eBook)
ISBN 978 1 80220 510 7 (paperback)

Printed and bound by CPI Group (UK) Ltd, Croydon, CR0 4YY

Contents

Acknowledgements

We gratefully acknowledge the support of the Erskine Visiting Fellows program of the University of Canterbury, and our sponsor Professor Tyron Love. In writing this book we entered into wonderful conversations with faculty, such as Professor Bryce Williamson (Dean Post Graduate Research), and Emeritus Professor Andy Pratt who taught about Karl Popper, and led us to inspiring documents such as the Canterbury Declaration. Many wonderful University of Canterbury doctoral students helped us find materials and helped us to refute our own theories and frameworks, thereby enabling self-correcting induction to happen. Sabrina Daddar was instrumental in checking out all eight volumes of the Collected Papers of Charles Sanders Peirce and is doing a dissertation using self-correcting storytelling. In addition, Mark van der Klei checked out 10 Karl Popper books and did a wonderful rendition of the self-correcting method. Sabrina Daddar and Mark, along with Mabel Sanchez, TK Thomas Kleiner, Jim Sibel, and Russ Barnes have done dissertations using self-correcting storytelling science, and are writing something about the process. Also, we appreciate all the help we received from the Christchurch community. Thanks to Ross Milne for helping David with the ensembles of multiplicities of Jean Paul Sartre so he could contrast it with Deleuzian multiplicities. Thanks to Professors Colleen Mills, Chris Chen, Fleur Pawsey, and the entire Management, Marketing and Entrepreneurship department at the University of Canterbury, and our Erskine Fellow sponsor, Associate Dean of Māori studies, Professor Tyron Love. We also appreciate the support of all our colleagues in Denmark, especially those at Aalborg University, as well as others at the University of Southern Denmark. Finally, we thank Jens Larsen and Lena Bruun Jensen for their work with David on their forthcoming book together on True Storytelling that features self-correcting storytelling science, which has helped our progress with the current volume.

David Boje and Grace Ann Rosile
10 February 2020

1. Introduction, brief history, topics addressed, how to use this book, and glossary of terms

We propose 'conversational storytelling interviewing' (CSI) as an alternative to semi-structured interviewing. Within 'storytelling science', conversational storytelling is part of a research methodology called 'self-correcting induction'.

In this book, we will explore how induction is part of the 'self-correcting' triad known as 'Abduction-Induction-Deduction' (AID) and is not just induction alone. Abduction is an intuitive, 'hunch' type of hypothesis, to which we then apply Induction tests of sampled cases so that we can make statements about a population. Deduction starts with theory, then draws hypotheses from theory, then tests the hypotheses by using data and cases.

By using all three of these AID forms of inquiry, the research reflects back on itself and allows for corrections and attunements at each stage. This is why AID is called a 'self-correcting' method. In some ways, 'self-correcting' is like a revival of formerly popular 'pilot studies', here more formalized and integrated as part of the storytelling science research process. This book will help you to both understand and apply these AID and self-correcting methods in your own research.

HISTORY

The classic Hawthorne Studies were transformed when, in July of 1929, after 1,600 interviews, they halted the project, and changed their interviewing method away from semi-structured and structured interviews. They replaced the 'direct approach to questioning' with the new 'indirect approach' in which people told their accounts and stories in conversations, without interruption, without the interviewer trying to herd the (*storyteller*) back to some *a priori* topics and sub-topics (Roethlisberger et al. 1939: 203). This indirect approach is what we (David and Grace Ann, in this book) now call '***conversational storytelling interviewing***' **(CSI)**. This indirect method was found to produce fewer social desirability effects. Instead of semi-structured interviews, the Hawthorne psychologists and psychoanalysts recommended a purposive storytelling conversation.

It is time to move beyond current over-reliance on semi-structured interviewing as a very limited business storytelling and social science methodology. We recommend a shift towards CSI. CSI combines classic 'indirect' storytelling interviewing, and incorporates dialogical and dialectical methods along with the AID 'self-correcting' cycles. This provides a very comprehensive and robust method. CSI also offers a personally meaningful and satisfying experience for both interviewees as well as interviewer researchers, as several successfully defended PhDs can attest.

TOPICS ADDRESSED

We will begin by answering the question: What is storytelling? We will look at the dialogical as well as dialectical dimensions of conversations. We introduce four (4) types of tests that may be applied in the self-correcting process. Then we offer a case example of using the AID process and the four (4) types of test that can be applied. We offer a 'storytelling paradigm' which positions self-correcting inductions within the context of theories, methodologies, and interventions relevant to 'storytelling science'. We address the entire dissertation research process, from choosing your topic and writing your theory and methods sections, through to managing your oral exams and post-submission job processes.

We discuss both quantitative and qualitative induction. We consider the metaphysics of storytelling science, and address both antenarrative and anti-narrative. We position CSI within the context of other approaches such as Grounded Theory, 4th Wave Grounded Theory, Appreciative Inquiry, and the Socio-Economic Approach to Management (SEAM) (Boje 2016d; Boje and Cai-Hillon 2017).

FORMAT: HOW TO USE THIS BOOK

This user-friendly book allows both the novice and the experienced storytelling researcher to find value. For the novice there is a helpful Glossary of Terms, organized by topic and also alphabetically indexed. For those more advanced or aspiring to become advanced, in each chapter, selected topics are explored in the 'In Depth' sections. In addition, each chapter has activities and/ or questions for self-reflexivity in the 'Exercise' boxes. Some of these activities may be done alone, some with a partner or partners, and some are suited for groups. All have been used successfully in either workshops or classrooms.

GLOSSARY OF TERMS GROUPED BY TOPIC

(See below this list for terms organized alphabetically and numbered 1–32.)

Abduction, Induction, Deduction, Self-correcting Method

1. **Abduction (#1 below)**: The 'A' in the AID (Abduction, Induction, Deduction) process; an intuitive guess, a tentative hypothesis, or speculative insight about what is being studied.
2. **Induction (#16 below)**: Gather qualitative or quantitative empirical data, and from that data develop generalizations and theories (thus going from observation to theory).
3. **Deduction (#7 below)**: The process in which a researcher starts with an existing theory, then uses the theory to develop a hypothesis about what is being studied, then tests the hypothesis to support or refute the theory (thus going from theory/hypothesis to testing/observation).
4. **Self-Correcting Method (#23 below)**: Using Abduction, Induction, and Deduction (AID) together in research. By this self-correcting learning by trial and error using the scientific method, we arrive closer to the truth (Popper 1963: 318).

Abstracting, Grounding

5. **Abstracting (#2 below)**: Reducing place, context, and change to universals or generalizations. *Abstracting* in Western narrative, reduces time to linear (beginning, middle, and end), develops a few events and characters to stand for the whole historical detail, and reduces place to spatial concepts rather than nature and community specificity. Abstracting and 'grounding' are aspects of a vertical axis of storytelling (see grounding).
6. **Grounding (#14 below)**: Vertical axis of storytelling, 'grounding' is contextual, about specifics of place, its nature, community, and living stories. (See abstracting.)
7. **True Storytelling (#31 below)**: An ethics approach to arriving closer to truth.

Antenarrative, Six Bs of Antenarrative, Linguistic Turn, Sociomaterialism, Narrative, Storytelling, Storytelling Organization, TamaraLand

8. **Antenarrative (#3 below)**: What comes before the story is constituted as 'the story'. Processes which are (pre)constitutive of both narratives and stories. Vertical axis antenarrative processes include 'abstracting' (typical of narrative-counternarrative that is often placeless), and 'grounding' in place (characteristic of indigenous living stories). Horizontal axis antenarrative processes include 'futuring' (prospective sensemaking, scenarios), and rehistoricizing (retrospective sensemaking narratives). (See Six Bs of Antenarrative.)

9. **Six Bs of Antenarrative (#24 below)**: Before, beneath, bets on the future, becoming, between, and beyond. Before (forehaving), beneath (foreconcepts), bets on the future (foresight), becoming (forecaring), between (forestructuring in advance), and beyond (foregrasping by intuition).

10. **Linguistic Turn (#18 below)**: In the 1970s, humanities and social sciences made a shift based on the claim of the primary importance of language in meaning-making and narrative. A countermovement, called socio-material, has claimed the linguistic turn went too far in dismissing the material aspects in the ontology of meaning-making. (See Sociomaterialism, Ontology, Narrative.)

11. **Sociomaterialism (#27 below)**: The entanglement of the social with materiality.

12. **Narrative (#20 below)**: Since Aristotle (350 BCE), narrative to be coherent has a beginning, middle, and end (linear time), with six elements (in order of importance): plot, characters, theme, dialogue, rhythm, and spectacle. Recently, spectacle has taken first place. Narrative requires story to be '... a whole ... a whole is that which has beginning, middle, and end' (Aristotle, 350 BCE: 1450b: 25, p. 233). Kenneth Burke (1945) renamed Aristotle's (350 BCE) narrative form elements and reduced them to five in his Pentad version. Act (plot), actor (characters), purpose (theme), agency (dialogue + rhythm), scene (spectacle). 'Typically searching for a causal chain', 'the plot follows – either the sequence beginning-middle-end or the sequence situation-transformation-situation. But sequence is the source of sense' (Weick 1995: 128). Czarniawska (1998: 78), for example, says narrative, or 'a *story* consists of a plot comprising causally related episodes that culminate in a solution to a problem'. Elsewhere, Czarniawska (1998: 2) clarifies, 'for them to become a narrative, they require a *plot*, that is, some way to bring them into a meaningful whole'.

13. **Storytelling (#28 below)**: The general term for the whole field, including Grand Narratives as well as Microstoria, and also including the pre-constitutive elements of storytelling called 'antenarrative' (Boje, 2001).

14. **Storytelling Organization (#29 below)**: Storytelling organizations are defined as multi-voices, multi-stylistic, multi-medium, and multi-languaged, and out of this heteroglot, storytelling organization can emerge.

15. **TamaraLand (#30 below)**: Boje's (1995) metaphor for the Storytelling Organization. 'Tamara' was a play by John Krizanc performed in a mansion in Los Angeles. The scenes from the play occurred simultaneously in many rooms, and the audience moved from room to room observing different parts of the story. The audience members never see the 'whole' story at once. Boje says this is what storytelling in organizations is like.

Auxiliary Assumptions, Fallibilism

16. **Auxiliary Assumptions (#4 below)**: Assumptions which underlie our hypothesis and can affect the outcomes of our hypothesis testing. Predictions come not only from a deductive theory on abductive-intuition (or hypothesis), but also come from other theories and assumptions, which are called 'auxiliary assumptions.' Auxiliary assumptions preclude Popper's absolute falsification of a deductive theory or induction-intuition: 'How can one determine whether a theory is falsifiable? The way to do this is to attempt to make predictions from the theory and see if these predictions have the possibility, at least in principle, of being shown to be wrong' (Trafimow 2009: 504).

17. **Fallibilism (#12 below)**: Error is possible because no theory (deduction), thesis (or antithesis), or abduction (inspiration) can be absolutely empirically proven, since there are always auxiliary assumptions (as well as Kant's citing of transcendental and moral reason issues) that have not been accounted for. (See Auxiliary Assumptions.)

'Big S' Science, 'Little s' Science

18. **'Big S' science (#5 below)**: 'Big S' science is communal, somewhat bureaucratic evolution of knowledge; 'little s' science is more speculative, more local, and more a 'Native Science' inquiry. Rather than either/or, we contend it is possible to do both/and, *both* 'big S' *and* 'little s' science.

19. **'Little s' science (#19 below)**: More about local knowing, being, and doing in a situation of place, in IWOK ('Indigenous Ways of Knowing'). (See 'Big S' science, IWOK.)

Conversational Interviewing, Dialogical, Dialectical, Social Heteroglossia

20. **Conversational Interviewing (#6 below)**: a back-and-forth exploratory process needed for self-correcting. This back-and-forth can be dialogical, involving sharing and exploring, and it can also be dialectical, with counternarratives (narratives which tell a different story) to the originally expressed narrative.

21. **Dialogical (#8 below)**: The way that communication between two or more people goes back-and-forth in a non-adversarial way that builds rapport and relationships. It may be confrontative, but typically in a win-win collaborative type of confrontation rather than a win-lose process. There are several dialogisms, the most known is polylogical (many logics), and polyphonic (many voices). Other dialogisms include stylistics (architectural, oral, written texts), chronotopes (nine spacetime relationships in the history

of the novel), and architectonics (interanimation of cognitive, aesthetic, and ethics discourses).

22. **Dialectical (#9 below)**: There are two types of dialectic. First, and most known, is the *thesis-antithesis-synthesis* (TAS) dialectic that tends to dualize into opposite polarized perspectives. TAS is often a dynamic of narrative-counternarrative dialectics. Second is the *'negation of the negation'* (N/N) that is more dialogical, with many perspectives.

23. **Social Heteroglossia (#26 below)**: The dialogical opposition of centripetal (centralization) forces with centrifugal (decentralization) forces of language and ideological-discourse.

Entanglement, Quantum Storytelling, Spacetimemattering

24. **Entanglement (#10 below)**: This refers to quantum-ness, where space and time and matter overlap with each other, and are therefore inseparable. (See Spacetimemattering.)

25. **Quantum Storytelling (#22 below)**: The entanglement of spacetimemattering (their inseparability) in Being (see Ontology), and 'grounding' in place, in nature, and community. (See Grounding.)

26. **Spacetimemattering (#25 below)**: The quantum view that space and time and matter overlap (are entangled) with each other.

Epistemology, Ontology

27. **Epistemology (#11 below)**: How we know what we think we know. Ways of knowing.

28. **Ontology (#21 below)**: Metaphysics branch focused on 'nature of Being'. Being is usually capitalized to differentiate from beings (living beings). Ways of Being-in-the-world (Heidegger 1927/1962). Spacetimemattering Being-in-the-world. (See spacetimemattering.)

4th Wave Grounded Theory, Grounded Theory

29. **4th Wave Grounded Theory (#13 below)**: This uses AID in self-correcting cycles; starts with Abduction before moving to Induction, then either revises Induction or moves to the Deduction phase of hypothesis testing. Then the cycle may loop back to Abduction, Induction, or Deduction for another cycle.

30. **Grounded Theory (#15 below)**: An 'inductive' research process that begins with observations and data collection, and from that develops theory (Glaser and Strauss 1967); often used in qualitative research. Grounded Theory has gone through four waves of development. 1st Wave embraces crude induction, and swallows the inductive fallacy whole. 2nd Wave Grounded Theory (Strauss and Corbin 1990; 1994/1998; Corbin and

Strauss 2007) tries to compensate by turning to empirical coding of the theme-forms into categories (typologies) using (post) positivism. 3rd Wave Grounded Theory (or 'constructivist Grounded Theory') departs from 1st Wave and 2nd Wave Grounded Theory by claiming that both theories and date are not discovered, but are constructed by the researcher in their interactions with the field of scholarship. 4th Wave includes process of self-correcting cycles. (See 4th Wave, Self-Correcting Method.)

IWOK, WWOK

31. **IWOK (#17 below)**: 'Indigenous Ways of Knowing', based on indigenous ontology, epistemology, and 'Native Science'; views all plants, animals, and the earth and streams as living beings interconnected with humans. Nature is the source of wisdom for humans. The way to knowledge is to study nature and observe the dynamics of the constant flux and interconnectedness of life.
32. **WWOK (#32 below)**: Western Ways of Knowing, based on Euro-Western ontology and epistemology; tends to see humans as separate from, and superior to, the rest of life and the planet. The way to knowledge is to immobilize, break apart, experiment, and take a snapshot of phenomena.

CROSS-INDEX OF TERMS ORGANIZED ALPHABETICALLY

(See above for term definitions.)

1. **Abduction**: See #1 above.
2. **Abstracting**: See #5 above.
3. **Antenarrative**: See #8 above.
4. **Auxiliary Assumptions**: See #16 above.
5. **'Big S' science**: See #18 above.
6. **Conversational Interviewing**: See #20 above.
7. **Deduction**: See #3 above.
8. **Dialogical**: See #21 above.
9. **Dialectical**: See #22 above.
10. **Entanglement**: See #24 above.
11. **Epistemology**: See #27 above.
12. **Fallibilism**: See #17 above.
13. **4th Wave Grounded Theory**: See #29 above.
14. **Grounding**: See #6 above.
15. **Grounded Theory**: See #30 above.
16. **Induction**: See #2 above.
17. **IWOK**: See #31 above.

18. **Linguistic Turn**: See #10 above.
19. **'Little s' science**: See #19 above.
20. **Narrative**: See #12 above.
21. **Ontology**: See #28 above.
22. **Quantum Storytelling**: See #25 above.
23. **Self-Correcting Method**: See #4 above.
24. **Six Bs of Antenarrative**: See #9 above.
25. **Spacetimemattering**: See #26 above.
26. **Social Heteroglossia**: See #23 above.
27. **Sociomaterialism**: See #11 above.
28. **Storytelling**: See #13 above.
29. **Storytelling Organizations**: See #14 above.
30. **TamaraLand:** See #15 above.
31. **True Storytelling**: See #7 above.
32. **WWOK**: See #32 above.

2. Dialogical and dialectical conversational interviews, and using self-correcting AID phases and 4 Tests with the CIW case example

WHY CONVERSATIONAL STORYTELLING IS BETTER THAN SEMI-STRUCTURED INTERVIEWING

We introduced the Hawthorne Studies in Chapter 1. Recall that the researchers conducting the Hawthorne Studies (initiated in July of 1929), halted their project after 1,600 interviews. At that point, they changed their interviewing method away from the semi-structured and structured interviews they called the 'direct approach to questioning' and instead adopted what they called the 'indirect approach'. With the indirect approach, people told their accounts and stories without interruption, without the researchers trying to herd the conversation back to some *a priori* topics and sub-topic themes (Roethlisberger et al. 1939: 203).

By October 1929, a second change in *conversation* was initiated. Instead of taking notes on the positive or negative statements made regarding the *a priori* topics of supervision, working conditions, and company (and their subthemes), the interviewer became a *listener*. As listeners, the interviewers took verbatim notes on all topics that the participant brought up, using what we now call a 'non-specific questioning' technique. This technique has long been used, as evident in the decades of work by Henri Savall on the Socio-economic Approach to Management (SEAM). SEAM does conversational storytelling by just listening with hardly any questions at all, just writing notes, to show you really care to listen (Boje 2016b; 2017b; 2019b; Cai-Hillon, Kisiel and Hillon 2016).

Consider these instructions to interviewers (from Roethlisberger et al. 1939: 534):

1. 'The [*conversationalist*] should listen not only to what a person wants to say but also for what he does not want to say or cannot say without help.'

2. The [*conversationalist*] should treat the mental contexts described in the preceding rule as indices and seek through them the personal reference that is being revealed.

From these new [*conversational*] methods it was concluded that the ideology expressed by workers was 'not based upon a logical appraisal of their situation' and that they were 'not acting strictly in accordance with their economic interests.'

CONVERSATIONAL STORYTELLING: MAKING IT DIALECTICAL AND DIALOGICAL, AND NOT THE OPPRESSIVE OPPOSITES

Let David be blunt, 'semi-structured interviews are the tool and apparatus of cultural invasion, conquest, colonization, and manipulation that entrap both oppressor and oppressed'. Its structured-ness keeps Grounded Theory from finding *ground* and *theory* of *praxis* of liberation via the paths of dialogic communication and dialectical self-correction. And as Linda Hitchin (2015) points out, it keeps the 'untold story' in a cell of silence, or in fear of 'living story' liberation. In contrast to oppressive structuring, Bakhtin (1981) describes polyphonic dialogism as being fully in one's own dialogical standpoint, while in a sacred space of listening, sharing, but not persuading by interrogation.

We can help to avoid oppressive structuring by making our conversations dialogical and dialectical. Storytelling conversations of self-correcting 'little s' science are both dialogical and dialectical. Semi-structured interviews can be anti-dialogical and anti-dialectical. Our glossary provides simple definitions of how we use these terms:

> **Dialogical**: The way that communication between two or more people goes back-and-forth in a non-adversarial way that builds rapport and relationships. It may be confrontative, but typically in a win-win collaborative type of confrontation rather than a win-lose process. There are several dialogisms, the most known is polylogical (many logics), and polyphonic (many voices). Other dialogisms include stylistics (architectural, oral, written texts), chronotopes (nine spacetime relationships in the history of the novel), and architectonics (interanimation of cognitive, aesthetic, and ethics discourses).
>
> **Dialectical**: There are two types of dialectic. First, and most known, is the *thesis-antithesis-synthesis* (TAS) dialectic that tends to dualize into opposite polarized perspectives. TAS is often a dynamic of narrative-counternarrative dialectics. Second is the '*negation of the negation*' (N/N) that is more dialogical, with many perspectives and directions.

In simple terms, dialogue means conversation, and conversation means that each participant's ideas connect to the previously-expressed idea or ideas. Thus, a conversation or a dialogue progressively builds and expands or develops meaning. One specific way in which meaning is developed may be through the contrast of opposing ideas, as in the TAS process, or the more subtle and diffuse 'negation of the negation'.

Later, we will expand our understanding of these terms. For the moment, we will consider the simple cases where a dialogue (conversation) may be further developed, or it may be inhibited, by various ways of conducting simple dialectic compare-and-contrast. Our purpose with conversational interviewing is to avoid the anti-dialogical and the anti-dialectical, in favor of dialogical and dialectical. Next we explain some of these differences.

One key difference we find in the work of Paulo Freire (1970/2000), on '*Conscientização*' inquiry into the situation of the entanglement of oppressor and oppressed. '*Conscientização*' is 'critical consciousness' that addresses 'fear of freedom' and a 'search for self-affirmation and thus avoids fanaticism by placing the status quo in question' (Freire 1970/2000: 36). We all understand that as a researcher, we want to question. We also understand that we do not want to become the oppressor, consciously or unconsciously imposing our views on the research. We avoid unintentionally becoming the oppressor through enhanced awareness. '*Conscientização*' is a methodology in generative storytelling conversations of self-correcting by a 'deepening attitude of awareness characteristic of all emergence' (Freire 1970/2000: 109).

Conscientização methodology **of** *conversational storytelling* **is back-and-forth, listening and telling.** Similarly, the theory of dialogical action has the following characteristics (see also Table 2.1):

1. Cooperation
2. Unity
3. Organization, and
4. Cultural synthesis

In contrast, Freire (1970/2000) proposes four ways that anti-dialogical action takes place:

1. Conquest
2. Divide and rule
3. Manipulation, and
4. Cultural invasion

Table 2.1   *Conscientização and the relation of dialectical and dialogical to their opposites with conversational storytelling*

	Dialectical	**Anti-Dialectical**
Dialogical	Conversational storytelling	Domesticated dialectic
	Conscientização	Truncated discussion leading to the
	Co-sharing	parties agreeing to disagree
	Co-inquiry	Listening without co-inquiry
	Double movement of dialectical and dialogical	Parallel conversations which do not engage the other
	Māori kōrero	Not braiding conversations between
	Indigenous ways of knowing (IWOK)	*Western Ways of Knowing* (WWOK) and
	'Native Science'	IWOK
	Freeing the Pedegogy of both oppressor and oppressed	Disappearance of social structure and social conditions of co-inquiry
Anti-Dialogical	Not listening to the Other	Semi-structured interviews reduce the
	Polemical	*concrete* to the *abstract confirmation* of
	WWOKers not entering space of	themes and subthemes
	co-sharing and co-inquiry	Perry-Mason-type cross examination to
	IWOKers remaining voiceless	support a pre-determined conclusion, as,
		for example, "Isn't it true that you…"
		It is the crisis *Western Ways of Knowing (WWOK)*

EXERCISE 2.1   CONVERSATIONAL STORYTELLING PRACTICE

FIRST ROUND

1. (1 min) Pick a Partner, choosing someone you know **least** well in the room. Decide who is Partner A and who is Partner B.
2. Write verbatim notes as you listen to each other.
3. **(1 min) Partner B: Share an experience of a BEST CONVERSATION** you have had, while Partner A takes notes.
4. (1 min) **Partner A: Share one of your own stories/memories, which could be a <u>counter-story</u>, triggered in your memory by B's story.** Then you (Partner A) tell the story you originally planned to tell (Step 5).
5. **(1 min) Partner A: Share an experience of a BEST CONVERSATION** you have had, while Partner B takes notes.
6. After the conversation is done, write up your critical reflections of your own storytelling, and your partner's storytelling.

SECOND ROUND

1. Pick a new Partner you know least in the room. Decide who is A and who is B.
2. Write verbatim notes as you listen to each other.
3. This time, **Partner A: Share an experience of a WORST CONVERSATION** you have had.
4. Follow Steps 4, 5, and 6 above, with the topic of WORST CONVERSATIONS.

Debrief After Both of the Two Rounds Are Complete

In pairs or foursomes, take turns answering the following questions:

1. What was the effect on each partner when the counterstories were offered by the other? Did it make a difference whether the counterstories were similar to the originating story or questioning/negating the originating story? Explain.
2. Was it easier to talk about the 'best' conversations or the 'worst' conversations?
3. What specific comments did you feel fostered a dialogical back-and-forth of conversation?
4. What specific comments did you feel fostered a dialectical exploring of other ideas?
5. Which was more comfortable, dialogical or dialectical?
6. Which generated the most valuable information, dialogical or dialectical?
7. From this exercise, could you draw any conclusions about what fosters and what restricts conversations?

Semi-structured interviewing, if we apply Freire (1970/2000), can be an interrogation method of 'non-communicative' (p. 109), 'oppressor action' (p. 135) with the 'aim of concurring them', and can take forms ranging from the 'most repressive to the most solicitous (paternalism)' (p. 138). The 'anti-dialogical' (p. 140) preserves 'the status quo' (p. 145) with the four anti-dialogic actions of conquest, divide and conquer, manipulation, and cultural invasion of colonizers. Dialogical conversational storytelling is liberation by back-and-forth co-inquiry into 'liberating action' (p. 139) from an 'oppressive reality.'

CONVERSATIONAL STORYTELLING INTERVIEWING AND THE AID TRIAD

What does all this discussion of dialectical and dialogical mean for story-telling conversational interviewing? We summarize five main points from the above discussion of conversational storytelling interviewing:

1. It needs to be a back-and-forth, or else it risks becoming interview-by-interrogation.
2. It needs to be dialogical or it risks reducing dialogism to monological narrative fallacy.
3. It needs to be dialectical, not just '*thesis-antithesis-synthesis*' (TAS) narrative-counternarrative oppositions done in semi-structured interviews.
4. It is a way to study multiplicity ensembles. Nature is a multiplicity of species, and we err in treating life as humancentric (speciesism) when a 'multispecies storytelling' (Haraway 2016) of ensembles of many kinds of life is possible.
5. It has to be not just Induction, but must include Abduction and Deduction (AID).

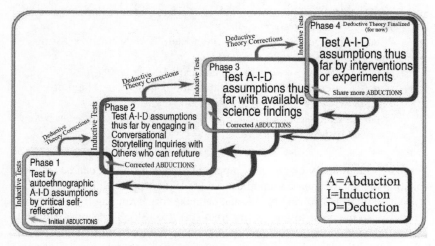

Figure 2.1   Self-correcting phases of 'storytelling science'

In each self-correcting phase of 'storytelling science' there is a cycle of Abduction-Induction-Deduction (AID) (see Figure 2.1). Each 'storytelling conversational interview' begins with Abductions (preliminary ideas) that are explored in the interview with Induction inference inquiry. Either from the beginning, or after the first cycle, there is Deduction from theories and from theorizing, followed by adjustments leading to new Abductions, then a second cycle with more Induction, all continuing in each self-correcting cycle.

In Depth: Using Abduction, Induction, and Deduction with Conversational Storytelling

For conversational storytelling to be a part of a rigorous researcher process, we recommend doing 'self-correcting induction'. This methodology is rooted in the work of Charles Sanders Peirce (1933–1937: 5.580, which hereafter means Volume 5, section 580, boldness ours): **'In an induction we enlarge our sample for the sake of the self-correcting effect of the induction.'** Just before this statement, Peirce (1933–1937: 5.579) amplifies his enthusiasm, 'So it appears that this marvelous self-correcting property of Reason, which Hegel made so much of, belongs to every sort of science, although it appears as essential, intrinsic, and inevitable only in the highest type of reasoning, which is induction.'

Understanding the AID process is important because it is in Volume 5, section 580 that Peirce (1931/1960) actually uses the term 'self-correcting effect of the induction'. That said, we must reiterate, it is only one part of the triad that Peirce is developing in his writing about the AID triad. We discuss this further in the sections addressing the Māori concept of 'braiding' theories, and also in the discussions of 'little s' science and 'Big S' science.

HOW CONVERSATIONAL STORYTELLING INTERVIEWS ARE SELF-CORRECTING USING AID PHASES AND THE 4 TESTS: THE CIW CASE EXAMPLE

The conversational storytelling interviewing research process is not the usual gathering of a bunch of semi-structured interviews, then transcribing them, and coming up with a theme analysis to generate a typology (aka taxonomy). Rather, it is back-and-forth storytelling conversational sharing, where you actually write down your *abductive-hypotheses BEFORE* the storytelling conversation (or participative immersion or experiment or intervention) and then do the inductive inquiry of the co-sharing storytelling (back-and-forth).

Next, we offer a detailed case example to demonstrate the process of self-correcting storytelling research. In this example we show four phases. Below, we give an example of each phase based on our (Rosile, Boje, and Claw 2018; Rosile et al. 2020 forthcoming) research on the Coalition of Immokalee Workers (CIW). These phases are summarized in Figure 2.2.

How is a research topic born? Much research begins with auto-ethnographic experiences with the topic, AID assumptions, hunches, what you (the researcher) sense is missing, overlooked, misunderstood, undervalued, or completely absent in the literature. What was the trigger that first led you to think 'I am curious, I want to study THAT'. We believe this pre-work is an important part of Abduction. We begin our CIW example with a recounting of the abductive processes that initiated this research.

Before we (David and Grace Ann) had even heard of the CIW, we (Rosile, Boje, and Claw 2018) had just completed an article on an egalitarian leadership model which we called Ensemble Leadership Theory (ELT). When Grace Ann presented this ELT work at a conference, a colleague (Rick Herder) started a conversation with Grace Ann. 'The group whose communication patterns I studied for my dissertation uses your ELT! In fact, their motto is "We are all leaders".'

Grace Ann wanted to know 'What exactly do they do on a daily basis to enact this motto?' We discussed what Rick had observed about this group. This was an informal conversational storytelling interview. Rick would say 'When the press wanted to interview their "leader" the CIW sent someone different each time'. I would respond with something like 'Yes, that is Ensemble, because ...' offering a complementary (agreeing) story. When Grace Ann said 'We found Ensemble processes in archeological accounts of Mesoamerica' Rick responded with another complementary story: 'Those are the ancestors of the Mexicans and Guatemalans in the CIW!' So, as often happens, Abduction slipped easily into Induction and Deduction in our conversation.

Rick Herder became Grace Ann's point of entry into the topic, even though he warned that the CIW were shy of outsiders and that all his dissertation work was done as an outside observer. Our abductive hunch was: The CIW constitutes a living and successful (for over 20 years) example of Ensemble Leadership. Now we began what we call our 'Pre-study' work.

Pre-Study Work. As Rick Herder had warned us, getting inside the CIW did not prove to be as easy as we expected. Grace Ann conducted conversational interviews (by phone) with a faith-based ally of the CIW, Rev. Noelle Damico, and some lay activists from the local community in South Florida, and finally an actual CIW member. Grace Ann believes the only reason this string of contacts led us to more contacts and eventually to the CIW was because of a long email in which Grace Ann introduced the group of researchers. She discussed their (David's and Grace Ann's) own activism against outsourced sweatshops, efforts in favor of living wages, and other work with grassroots community members in Los Angeles and New Mexico. Basically, we shared our own personal stories. Our message was NOT: we are objective observers. Supposed 'objectivity' is a known deterrent to rapport and open conversations. Our message was: we are on your side, against abusive working conditions and in favor of fair living wages, and here is 20 years of our history of standing up for these things.

We had planned to study the CIW by going to their Florida headquarters and observing their organizational practices. This would be Induction, where we would observe what, if any, Ensemble behaviors the CIW enacted. It was not to be. The refusal was so polite we did not realize until later that it was, in fact, a refusal. Our CIW contact suggested that we travel to their big demonstration in Columbus, Ohio, to see them in action and learn what they were about, before visiting their headquarters. We were warned not to expect them to take time out for us, as all the CIW members would be very busy running the event. Grace Ann assured them we would be unobtrusive participant observers. We were in!

We already had a 'questionnaire' approved by our University's Institutional Research Board (IRB) even though we did not expect to be doing anything, at this stage, that might require IRB approval. One benefit of this IRB process was that we had already formulated Abductions regarding the egalitarian nature of the CIW. Our Abductions were reinforced by our Inductive data, such as reviews of news reports and the CIW's own web postings. Our Deductions regarding ELT were also confirmed by our initial conversations with those two external-to-the-CIW connections (faith-based and community-based).

Phase 1. Our research group was able to spend 3 days in Columbus. Among other things, we saw one of the 'founders' of the group sweeping the lunch-room floor on the first day, when the large meeting room was almost empty. Later we saw the same man (Lucas Benitez) serving burritos in the lunch line.

We were fortunate that our research team of three faculty and two students was able to stay together in a relative's house. Every morning over breakfast and every evening over dinner, we were able to discuss what we observed, and share our processes of co-inquiry. For example, we shared our various conversations with demonstration participants who had brought their primary-school-aged children, grandchildren, nieces, and nephews along. The adults said they took the children out of school, because this (demonstration) was important. This was a powerful statement about how the group established and reinforced the culture of solidarity. Our focus was beginning to shift from the presence or absence of indicators of leadership behaviors, to collective behaviors.

On another day in Columbus, during a break, Grace Ann asked our native-Spanish-speaking grad student to introduce us to an older gentleman who had been standing alone for a while. When our student spoke to him in Spanish, his previously-impassive features broke into a huge grin. In the course of conversation, we discovered he had left Mexico due to political persecution. He had been studying law. When we asked what he liked in his studies, he said the work of Antonio Gramsci. We said we all knew and admired Gramsci ourselves. There was a sudden feeling of comradeship. This conversation shifted our entire idea of who these agricultural workers were.

Specifically, what our observations there confirmed for us was our Induction, based on our observations (data), that this CIW group was truly an egalitarian organization, and not some hierarchical power structure that just 'talked nice' when telling people what to do. We had plenty of other inductive proof of our abductive hunch that this group was truly egalitarian. We were still in for a surprise at the next phase of the research.

Phase 2. After the Columbus 'participant observation' and informal 'conversational interviews', we realized only with hindsight that they were observing us at the same time that we were observing them. Shortly after the Columbus trip, we contacted them again regarding a visit to their headquarters. We were told our request would be brought up at the next Monday staff meeting. They would let us know their answer afterwards. (Aha! Was this an egalitarian decision-making process?) Apparently, we passed muster, and were invited to Florida to observe them at their headquarters for a week.

Arriving in Florida on a Sunday, Grace Ann asked to attend the Monday staff meeting, and was told no. However, she was invited to tag along on a typical trip for training workers in the fields about their rights through the CIW – if she did not mind leaving at 4:30 am. It was a wonderful trip and Grace Ann learned a lot, observing training taking place in the remote agricultural fields in both Spanish and Haitian languages. The two-hour drive each way to the fields that day, plus a lunch break at a restaurant, provided more opportunity for mutual story-sharing between Grace Ann and the CIW staff members.

Our next deductive step was to use our semi-structured interview questionnaire to determine if the CIW actually used ELT. We used the semi-structured interview format mostly as a back-up to our conversational interviews. However, it was needed in advance of our on-site research both for the IRB approval process and also to give the CIW some idea of what questions we might ask. In the end, we very rarely used the questionnaire. Most of our time for this project was spent as participant observers, and we just let people approach us (although sometimes we approached them) and let them tell us their stories in casual conversations, as we had done in Columbus.

When we did use the semi-structured question format, the results were not quite what we expected. For example, we asked Lucas Benitez: How do you motivate people? This elicited a surprisingly vehement response: No, we do not MOTIVATE people. We ANIMATE. We realized all our questions were stuck in a hierarchical model of leadership, assuming leaders 'motivate' followers. We were wrong. We had to correct some Abductions, as well as do some Deductive Theory Corrections. So we quickly reverted to conversational storytelling, and let Lucas tell us his stories in his own way.

A similar thing happened when there was an evening community meeting at the headquarters with refreshments served and about 25 to 30 people seated at long tables forming a big circle at the edges of the main meeting room. Rick Herder and Grace Ann were present, and took seats at what they thought was a darker spot at the tables. They were quietly and politely asked to move to the outer edges of the room, behind the seated participants. They were told the English speakers might inhibit the predominantly Spanish-speaking participants.

Again, we had inadvertently assumed positions of privilege, violating the egalitarian foundations of this organization. Staying in those seats would have certainly precluded co-inquiry. As it was, it seemed attendees were very quiet for the first 30 minutes, and only started to speak up in the final half-hour of the meeting. How do you study egalitarianism by unobtrusive observation when your very presence invokes hierarchy?

Finally, while in Florida, we discovered a whole different concept that was entwined with egalitarianism, solidarity, and an abuse-free workplace in the agricultural fields. This concept was called 'worker-driven social responsibility'. Through self-empowered solidarity, the CIW found that worker-driven processes were the best thus far, and perhaps the only proven way, to ensure an abuse-free work environment.

Phase 3. In this phase, our Spanish-speaking graduate student team member worked in the onion fields in New Mexico, to compare that experience with what was reported in Florida. One interesting observation came from her casual conversations with one woman co-worker. Note that these co-workers were mostly women, as onion harvesting is deemed an easier job suitable for women. After this field experience, our student received a text from the co-worker. It was a photo of one of the young men stopping to smoke a cigarette in the field. The woman onion-harvester joked: He's pretending to be a boss! The assumptions were that bosses don't work, they can afford to stand around and smoke cigarettes, and if you are an onion harvest worker you will not be seen standing idly in the fields smoking a cigarette. This is the view of what it means to be a 'boss'. In this onion field, petty harassments were common, such as asking repeatedly how many sacks of onions a worker had picked. This happened so often, our student felt like she was not believed and like she was losing track of the count herself. No one spoke against these behaviors. Would CIW members have reacted differently?

Phase 4. Finally, our student concluded that all the issues of abusive conditions in agricultural fields, including sexual harassment, related to the idea of 'dignity' as a worker's right. She will pursue this aspect of the research in California, where she has been offered a position after she completes her defense.

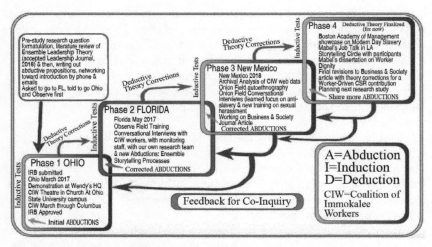

Figure 2.2   Self-correcting 'storytelling science'

The Deductions from theory are applied to your research situation, and come *BEFORE or AFTER* each round of conversational interviews. It is therefore inadequate to stick to a protocol of semi-structured questions, since the theory assumptions (deductions), the inquiry (induction), and the propositional assumptions (Abductions) can *CHANGE* from phase to phase.

The point we are making is to write out the Abductions-inductions-deductions as you go, not post hoc, after-the-fact.

Figure 2.2 shows phases of self-correcting as they relate to our CIW research, beginning with pre-research, then the Columbus, Ohio observations, the Florida on-site visit, then extending the work to New Mexico. Finally, we anticipate that our CIW co-researcher Mabel Sanchez will be continuing this work in California. At each phase, the AID process continues.

STORYTELLING SCIENCE FOUR TESTS

Conversational storytelling interviews can be self-correcting by involving up to four tests:

1. Refutation test of *self-reflexivity* involving *self-conversations,* which we now call autoethnography;
2. Storytelling *conversations with others to refute your own 'auxiliary assumptions'* (as our friend David Trafimow (2012) calls them);
3. *Understanding the science and processes of Nature* (and of other sciences) in relation to your research question;

4. *Doing experiments and interventions* to get your '*abstracting*' closer to '*grounding*'.

The above four tests are done (as needed) in each AID cycle of self-correcting storytelling science. In the CIW example above, our team of researchers used primarily Tests 1 and 2. The first test was a self-reflexivity with self-conversations test. We each individually questioned what we observed in a critical manner. Then we used Test 2, which was facilitated by us being a multi-researcher team. Further, we took advantage of ample opportunities during our travels and field work together, to converse about the research process and what we were observing as we were observing it (Test 2, storytelling with others to refute auxiliary assumptions).

Tests 3 and 4 refer to understanding the science, and doing experiments, respectively. For an example of the potential use of Test 3, consider our field-worker who had studied Gramsci. He told us about toxic chemicals used in the fields. The chemicals were sprayed too close in time and in distance from where workers were picking in that particular field, actually violating legal regulations. The bosses ignored complaints, and our worker ended up in the hospital for a week due to that toxic exposure. In this example, Test 3 could be applied relating to the scientific details regarding toxic agricultural chemicals and their regulation. Test 3 would be an appropriate test for this particular story example. Keep in mind, however, that scientific details need not be restricted to hard sciences. Social sciences may be tested as well. In the CIW example, the researcher can look to the social sciences regarding leadership to test the results of the research.

Test 4, experiments, are used extensively by Henri Savall's France-based institute using their SEAM organizational research and consulting process. For over 20 years with over 2,000 cases, they have called their organizational interventions 'experiments'. In our CIW research, our student's experiences in the New Mexico onion fields could be seen as constituting an experimental replication or a test of generalizability of our Florida findings.

In Figure 2.1, we saw that the four tests might be applied at successive stages of the research, if the world was logical and orderly. However, since this 'auxiliary assumption' of logic and order rarely holds, research projects will rarely look like this. The good news is that self-correcting science is ideally suited to an illogical, disorderly world, as it builds in course-correction-testing along the way. So returning to Figure 2.1, keep in mind that (a) all four tests need not be used; (b) tests might be used in a different order from what is shown; and (c) tests may be used in a cyclical sequence rather than a linear one.

For Popper, what Peirce calls self-correcting is termed the 'trial and error' of the scientific method, so we are in a continual process of arriving closer to the truth (Popper 1963: 318). Karl Popper, Charles Sanders Peirce, and our

French colleague, Henri Savall, are all in agreement about self-correcting as a science. These three all agree that *critical conversations* with *self* and with *others*, observations of *the multiplicities ensembles of nature*, and if all else fails, actual experiments and interventions in *praxis* are required to refute *fake storytelling* and get closer to the 'True Storytelling' (Boje, Larsen, and Bruun 2017; Larsen, Bruun, and Boje, *in press*) while maintaining the humility of *fallibilism*. Peirce (1933–1937: 1.141) says this about fallibilism:

> All positive reasoning is of the nature of judging the proportion of something in a whole collection by the proportion found in a sample. Accordingly, there are three things to which we can never hope to attain by reasoning, namely, absolute certainty, absolute exactitude, absolute universality. We cannot be absolutely certain that our conclusions are even approximately true; for the sample may be utterly unlike the unsampled part of the collection. We cannot pretend to be even probably exact; because the sample consists of but a finite number of instances and only admits special values of the proportion sought. Finally, even if we could ascertain with absolute certainty and exactness that the ratio of sinful men to all men was as 1 to 1; still among the infinite generations of men there would be room for any finite number of sinless men without violating the proportion. The case is the same with a seven legged calf.

For example, for the longest time, there was the theory and belief: '*all* swans are white', but it was refuted when in May 1934, in Vienna, a black swan stood between 10 and 11 am for all to see (Popper 1956/1983: xx). Fallibilism of certainty, exactitude, and universality is that about which 'little s' 'storytelling science' is self-critical, and self-reflexive about the metaphysics of its own assumptions.

In Depth: 'Little s' Science vs. 'Big S' Science

We intend a '*little s' science*, *instead of* '*Big S' S*cience. 'Big S' 'Science' was challenged by Jean-François Lyotard (1979/1984: 15, 37) with 'delegitimation and nihilism' and growing incredulity to the '*G*rand *N*arrative' of 'advanced [neo] liberal capitalism' in 'the partial replacement of teachers by machines' he found 'intolerable' and therefore gave credulity for 'breaking up of the grand Narratives' into 'thousands of little narratives'. Lyotard cites the work of Price and de Solla (1963): 'little science, Big Science'. There is ongoing hegemony between 'Big Science' and 'little science' as there is between 'Big Story' and 'little story'. Price and de Solla (1963: 2) note 'Big Science is so large that many of us begin to worry about the sheer mass of the monster we have created.' Our book explores two approaches to overcome the dualism of 'Big Story' over 'little story': (1) *dialogical*, following the work of Bakhtin (1981) and Freire (1970/2000); and (2) *dialectical*, which Freire also pursued, but differently than Bakhtin.

'Little s' 'storytelling science' in relation to 'Big S' 'Storytelling Science' is about the interplay of AID in relations of three kinds of induction. You have some idea to investigate, and this idea is an abductive-hypothesis that takes you on a journey of discovery. Peirce (1931/1960: 2.758–2.759) puts three kinds of induction in relationship:

1. **Crude Induction**: 'Future experience will not be utterly at variance with all past experience.' In storytelling, this is retrospective sensemaking narrative, where we take the messiness of life experience and organize it into neat linear plots, and then we expect those plots to continue into the future.
2. **Quantitative Induction**: 'What is the "real probability" that an individual member of a certain experiential class, say the S's class, will have a certain character, say that of being P?'
3. **Qualitative Induction**: This is an intermediate position between Crude and Quantitative Induction. 'Upon a collection of innumerable instances of equal evidential value, different parts of it have to be estimated according to our sense of the impression they make upon us.' This we first deduce from 'abductive' (or 'retroductive') hypothesis (terms he uses sometimes differently, other times interchangeably).

Our quotes from Peirce come from the eight volumes of *Collected Papers of Charles Sanders Peirce* (1931–1935; 1933–1937; 1958; 1931/1960). These volumes are by various editors. All of these editors have important things to say about deduction-induction-abduction ways of reasoning that can inform storytelling science. Since you may have any one of these collections or some other one, we cite the volume number and paragraph number so you can find the reference easily. For example 8.385 is Volume 8, section 385, and this next selection is from the 1958 collection.

Peirce (1958: 8.385) (see Figure 2.3) says since the 1860s he 'recognized three different types of reasoning:

> 1st *Deduction* which depends on our confidence in our ability to analyze the meanings of the signs in or by which we think;
> 2nd *Induction*, which depends upon our confidence that a run of one kind of experience will not be changed or cease without some indication before it ceases; and
> 3rd *Retroduction [aka Abduction]*, or Hypothetic Inference, which depends on our hope, sooner or later, to guess at the conditions under which a given kind of phenomenon will present itself.'

Next we consider how to choose a thesis for your conversational storytelling dissertation research. We consider the research question, your investigative methods, and your choice of storytelling paradigm. We include discussion of

Quantum Storytelling, Narrative-Counternarrative, Living Story, and Narrative Retrospective Sensemaking, and Antenarrative Prospective Sensemaking.

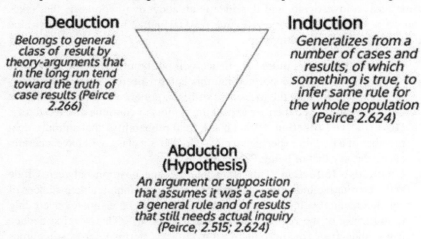

Deduction

Belongs to general class of result by theory-arguments that in the long run tend toward the truth of case results (Peirce 2.266)

Induction

Generalizes from a number of cases and results, of which something is true, to infer same rule for the whole population (Peirce 2.624)

Abduction (Hypothesis)

An argument or supposition that assumes it was a case of a general rule and of results that still needs actual inquiry (Peirce, 2.515; 2.624)

Figure 2.3   Peirce definitions of the ABDUCTION-INDUCTION-DEDUCTION (AID) Triad

3. Choosing your research question, and using the storytelling paradigm theories including narrative retrospective, antenarrative prospective, counternarrative, living story, ensemble storytelling, and Grounded Theory

In this chapter we consider how to choose a thesis for your conversational storytelling dissertation research. We present our Storytelling Research Paradigm organized according to Theory, Method, or *Praxes*. We consider the research question, and your choice within the storytelling paradigm of the particular theories you want to use. We include discussion of Quantum Storytelling, Narrative Retrospective and Antenarrative Prospective Sensemaking, Narrative-Counternarrative, Living Story, and Ensemble Leadership's Ensemble Storytelling. We emphasize self-correcting methods of induction throughout this chapter. We begin with how to use Abduction to focus in on your conversational storytelling research question.

CHOOSING YOUR RESEARCH QUESTION FOR CONVERSATIONAL STORYTELLING INTERVIEWING

Storytelling is the way we make sense of our lives. If we want to understand something about organizational life, conversational storytelling research is a good choice of method. This book will explain how philosophers and researchers back to Aristotle can help us to understand storytelling. Further, there is much we can learn from these earlier thinkers, as well as some more recent ones, about storytelling research. We can learn how to use storytelling to draw conclusions that go beyond the individual to give us insights about groups of people as they exist within their own contexts. If you want to do research as close to the lived experiences of real people without actually being there, this book can help you.

When a person 'tells their story', that story will change depending on how the person feels that day, depending on the time and place of the telling, depending on how the story itself wishes to be told, and very much depending on who is listening. In 'Conversational Storytelling', each party tells a piece of their story to the other, to build a trusting, reciprocal relationship. Note that we say 'piece of their story' because what we call 'living story' may be fragmented, still in flux, and intertwined with other pieces of other stories. This will be explained further in subsequent chapters.

Tell your dissertation story. Every part of your dissertation is an opportunity to tell a story worth telling. From the opening living story of why you love this topic, to the theories, methods, findings, and conclusions, you have opportunities to tell your story. You can choose to use Native Science and/or Western Science, and both are ways of storytelling. If we could go back in time to that place in our own doctoral education, we would learn how to do the both/and of 'little s' 'storytelling science' and 'Big S' 'Storytelling Science'.

David remembers the defining moment in his doctoral education when his mentor, Louis R. Pondy, said to David in the mid-1970s, 'Your best work is in storytelling.' With this book, we hope to expand the ways you can express your best work, whether quantitative or qualitative or both. You will also be able to position your storytelling work appropriately within 'small 's' storytelling science and/or 'Big S' Storytelling Science.

DO YOU CHOOSE THE LINGUISTIC TURN OR THE ONTOLOGICAL TURN?

We are coming out of a *'linguistic turn'* that has dominated 'storytelling science' far too long. We are grasping a pendulum turned to the constituting of the future. We write about what Lyotard (1979/1984: 22) calls 'little splinters of potential narratives' as *antenarrative processes, the splintering ante* (*before*), as (*bets on the future*), as (*between*), as (*beneath*), as (*becoming*) and (*beyond*) processes constituting narratives and stories. Boje (2001; 2008; 2019b) and Svane (2019) ask six B-questions based in Heidegger's (1923/1988/1999; 1927/1962; 2003) 'fore-notions' (discussed later in this chapter).

> **Language has been granted too much power**. The linguistic turn, the semiotic turn, the interpretative turn, the cultural turn: it seems that at every turn lately every 'thing' – even materiality – is turned into a matter of language or some other form of cultural representation. (Barad 2003: 801, boldness ours)

> We are intellectually, it may be said, the prisoners of our language: we cannot think except in terms of theories (of substance, or of space and time, for example) which, unknown to us, are incorporated in our language; and we cannot escape by our own efforts – for example by means of a critical discussion – from our prison, for the

critical discussion would have to be conducted with the help of our language; and it would therefore remain within the prison … It seems to me there that there is a great deal in this doctrine of imprisonment, but that its consequences are exaggerated … We may succeed in our own critical efforts in breaking down one or another of our prison walls… it largely consists in our intellectual blindness to the prison walls. (Popper 1956/1983: 16)

Moving away from the linguistic turn, the ***ontological turn*** is away from the belief that humans are the center of the universe to a posthumanistic ethics, a respect for all species to have what is needed to survive. Here are some summary points for would-be Baradians:

1. Barad uses a posthumanist storytelling of discursive practices and material-ity and the relationship between them, rather than just humanist accounts.
2. Barad's storytelling is agentive realism, when it is the *intra*-activity of materiality *with* discourse. It is never interaction, always intra-activity.
3. Barad's concept of 'ethico-onto-epistemological matter' (Barad 2008: 333) reflects her view of the inseparability of knowing-being-doing entanglements.
4. Barad treats duality as a both/and ontology and dualism as an either/or epistemology.
5. For Barad, there are agential cuts (dualities such as subject versus object, internal and external, animate and inanimate, space versus time, spacetime versus mattering) in following a research method or in telling a narrative or story, that create self and othering.

An apparatus (such as a research method, a survey, an interview protocol, a software for doing quantitative narrative analysis) makes agential cuts.

6. It is never space, time, matter for Barad, but rather the inseparability entan-glement of *spacetimemattering* in iterative reconfiguring.

We in this book will argue the Baradian *spacetimemattering entanglement of iterative configuring* relates to a new method, which was inspired in us by C. S. Peirce. We call this method ***self-correcting induction***, or what Popper calls correcting our fallibility by testing our conjectures of the new, while engaging in 'little s' 'science'. Put simply, instead of doing a bunch of interviews, and *post hoc* locking yourself in a room to fathom a typology, *in advance*, the researcher writes out abductive-hypotheses *ante-to-going to the field*. Then the researcher does a round of a few or several *storytelling conversations* of inductive inquiry, and writes up the findings, while being self-critical and self-reflexive about the deductions. This *abductive-inductive-deductive cycle* is done several times more until you have some confidence you have sampled enough to understand the population. This way you move from 'crude induction' to some combination of qualitative and quantitative induction. Qualitative induction in the self-correcting process is an exploration of the whole storytelling context.

WHAT IS YOUR RESEARCH QUESTION?

Your research question guides your research. Each research question is a different dissertation. It is best to have one solid research question to start with. Avoid the temptation to have several, as you may never finish. If you must have several, make the others subcomponents of the one main research question.

Arthur Schopenhauer (1788–1860) taught Nietzsche about 'will'. Schopenhauer (1928) can help you write a storytelling research question. Storytelling in its many fields has two kinds of will, a narrative form called morphology (idea-form types) and a mattering of change called etiology (study of cause and effect longitudinally, historically, and predictively). You can write a research question willfully inviting morphology or one inviting etiology. Keep in mind 'Modern pessimism is an expression of the uselessness of the modern world – not of the world of existence' (Nietzsche 1968: #34, p. 23).

In Depth: Morphology and Etiology

On the one hand, morphology is about classifying narrative-form themes and subthemes into general typologies of theme-ideas. On the other hand, etiology is about storytelling history into causes and effects in mythical narrative forces, as your explanation. These are different wills. Schopenhauer's morphology-will and etiology-will point to a storytelling of the human tragedy forms of existence wrought by Western Ways of Knowing (WWOK), and the potential Indigenous Ways of Knowing (IWOK) wisdom of life that keeps slipping away. Schopenhauer writes with pity about the ***morphology-will***, having awakened from romantic narrative fantasy to see the comedy narrative of errors of human activities impacting the world, and the irony of will of striving that never finds peace. The ***etiology-will*** searches for the law of cause and effect to find changing states of matter, in particular places and at particular times, derived from experience of the '*force of nature*' pointing to an 'environment of forces which cannot be explained' (Schopenhauer 1928: 60–1). Some do epistemology of classification imitating the mind of the 'winged cherub without a body'. Others do etiology as all body but no mind except the 'living story' mind of bodies in community and in movement, and in laws of nature encountered as unseen forces (p. 63). Speaking for myself (David), I choose with Schopenhauer (1928: 66) to 'analyze the reality of the body and its actions' and find 'nothing but the will'. Usually I find the Nietzschean will to power.

HOW DO YOU PROPOSE TO INVESTIGATE YOUR RESEARCH QUESTION?

This is where you design your research methodology. It can be qualitative, quantitative, or some combination. Methods of classification (disembodied narrative morphology) and methods of etiology (embodied ontology of cause and effect) history are different. Both can apply to quantitative research, and both are qualitative.

In choosing your research question, we recommend starting with Abduction, with your intuitive hunch about what is interesting to you. After you pick a subject area of interest, you will seek relevant theories suited to your topic. Once you have chosen your theories (discussed below as 'The Storytelling Research Paradigm') then you will design your method, which if you are reading this book, will be some version of conversational storytelling interviews in cycles of self-correcting induction.

To help you begin your abductive process to choose your research question, we offer this exercise to heighten awareness of the many ways Abductions are important to our research process.

EXERCISE 3.1   A CONVERSATIONAL INTERVIEW ABOUT ABDUCTION IN THE RESEARCH PROCESS

Abductions can range from an educated guess or an intuitive hunch, up to a wild guess, about a subject we want to study. But what if only some people are intuitive, or only some find Abduction useful? In Paris, David and Grace Ann asked a group of about a dozen ESCE (*Ecole Supérieure du Commerce Extérieur*) business school scholars, both qualitative and quantitative, if they could recall a time when Abduction (an intuitive hunch) helped them to progress in a research project. Everyone was able to do so, and with enthusiasm.

To start things off, Grace Ann gave the group her own example, which she tells you here in her own voice:

I was in my first Master's Program in Health Care Administration at the University of Pittsburgh's Graduate School of Public Health. I woke up one sunny spring morning with the persistent idea that I needed to take a class in 'Behavioral Science'. There was no 'dream' that I could recall, only this strange conviction. I was not even sure what 'Behavioral Science' was, but I must have heard the term somewhere. That led me to sign up for a class in Human Behavior in Organizations at Pitt's College of Business, which led to my subsequent PhD in Organizational Behavior.

Your assignment is to think of a time when an intuitive hunch or inspiration helped you through a difficult point in a research project. If you cannot think of a personal example, find another student or professor and ask them the question. (Remember that it is said that Albert Einstein read science fiction and also a philosopher who questioned the separation of time and space, perhaps contributing to his inspired scientific breakthroughs.) During or after this process, write down three Abductions.

THE STORYTELLING RESEARCH PARADIGM

We present our Storytelling Research paradigm, including Theory, Method, and *Praxes*, in Figure 3.1. This chapter will focus on Theory, as shown in Figure 3.2.

STORYTELLING PARADIGM	WESTERN WAYS OF KNOWING **WWOK**		INDIGENOUS WAYS OF KNOWING **IWOK**	
THEORY	Quantum Storytelling Theory			
	Narrative Retrospective Sensemaking	Narrative-Counternarrative Dialectics	Living Story Dialogisms	
			Ensemble Leadership Theory	
	Antenarrative Prospective Sensemaking			
	2nd Wave Grounded Theory	3rd Wave Grounded Theory	4th Wave Grounded Theory	1st Wave Grounded Theory
METHOD	Self-Correcting Induction Method			Crude Induction
	Quantitative Induction	Qualitative Induction		
	Narrative Quantification	Ethno-statistics	Qualimetrics	Critical Accounting
	Storytelling Multiplicities Analyses			
PRAXES	Socio-Economic Storytelling		Critical Accounts	Appreciative Inquiry
	Text-based Restorying	Embodied Restorying Process		
	True Storytelling			

Figure 3.1   The storytelling research paradigm

WHAT THEORIES WILL YOU USE AND CONTRIBUTE TO?

In Figure 3.2 we offer a framework of various storytelling theories. All are categorized according to whether they reflect WWOK or IWOK. Notice that Quantum Storytelling Theory and Antenarrative theory can be compatible with both WWOK and IWOK.

STORYTELLING PARADIGM	WESTERN WAYS OF KNOWING **WWOK**		INDIGENOUS WAYS OF KNOWING **IWOK**	
THEORIES	Quantum Storytelling Theory			
	Narrative Retrospective Sensemaking	Narrative-Counternarrative Dialectics	Living Story Dialogisms	
			Ensemble Leadership Theory	
	Antenarrative Prospective Sensemaking			
	2nd Wave Grounded Theory	3rd Wave Grounded Theory	4th Wave Grounded Theory	1st Wave Grounded Theory

Figure 3.2   What theories are in your 'storytelling science' paradigm?

Before you ask the question, we will answer: 'Yes, there are other theories'. This is only meant to be illustrative of how to choose storytelling theories.

QUANTUM STORYTELLING THEORY

What is the space, time, and mattering of Quantum Storytelling Theory? In Quantum Storytelling Theory, everything is connected to everything at an energy vibration level, such that ***spacetimemattering*** has no separations. It is quantum entanglement. Western science (Barad 2007) has undergone a paradigm shift where space, time, and mattering are no longer separated. Instead, they exist in entanglement, not separable into static categories. This is why Barad uses the quantum science term of *spacetimemattering*. Also, *Indigenous Science* (or Native Science) (Cajete 1994; 1999; 2000; 2015) has traditionally considered *spacetimemattering* as inseparable and entangled without using these terms.

The 'storytelling paradigm' shift from Cartesian-separations of space from time and mattering to its quantum entanglement is important to your dissertation. It is said in Quantum Storytelling (Boje 2014; Boje and Henderson 2014;

Boje 2016; Henderson and Boje 2016), you cannot simultaneously observe -by-measurement-apparatuses with equal accuracy the wave form and the particles simultaneously, in the same event. In Quantum Storytelling, the petrified unchanging bits of the well-formed narrative are like particles, and the evolving living stories are like waves. Both exist simultaneously in a dynamic interrelationship, but we may not be able to measure and observe both at the same time. When our storytelling looks forward or backward in time, the antenarrative (future sensemaking) and the retrospective (past sensemaking) are in a relationship that fits Neils Bohr's *Principle of Complementarity*.

Western narrative tends to look at time as linear, but indigenous storytelling sees time as a quantum dimension able to fold back on itself. Similarly, Western narrative views place as an inert 'setting' for a story, while indigenous storytelling recognizes place as an agential character in the story. In general, indigenous storytelling is more different from Western narrative, and is more similar to Quantum Storytelling and to Living Story (discussed later in this chapter).

Grace Ann says, 'Storytelling is really not about the story that is told, it is about the story that is elicited in others.' 'True Storytelling' is about telling a story from the part of our being-ness which is connected to others. That connectedness resonates, and it is what makes the story meaningful for the listeners. This is why some stories with ethical and moral lessons are remembered and repeated, and others are not. This is what great speakers do when they establish rapport with their audience: they elicit the feeling of recognition, of coming home, in the listeners. Such rapport can often come from the 'untold stories' (Hitchin 2015), so embedded in lived experience, that people don't tell them. These untold stories may be taboo topics that are repressed or marginalized in some way, or so obvious to insiders that they are taken-for-granted.

NARRATIVE-COUNTERNARRATIVE DIALECTICS

Bamberg and Andrews (2004: 1) defined counternarratives as a concept that 'only make sense in relation to something else, that which they are countering. The very name identifies it as a positional category, in tension with another category.' Narrative-counternarrative always has dialectic opposition (Boje, Gergerich, and Svane 2016; Boje, Svane, and Gergerich 2016), one that missed, or is blind to the surround of multiplicities in their dialogical ensembles (Bakhtin 1981; Gabriel 2016). There are several types (morphological forms) of 'dialectic'. One is the infamous *triadic* of *thesis-antithesis-synthesis*. Hannah Arendt (1978: 48–9) retheorizes the *triadic* into a series of *thesis-antithesis-synthesis* 'cycles of reticular progress' and 'dialectical movement' that become what we call antenarratively reconstituted out of 'cyclical time … forming a *Spiral*, (which) is grounded on the experiences of neither the thinking ego nor the willing ego' and 'gives to Future over the present and past' (Boje et al. 2017; Rosile et al. 2013).

Arendt's (1978) point is that thinking and willing have opposing time concepts (p. 117). We have redrawn it as in Figure 3.3.

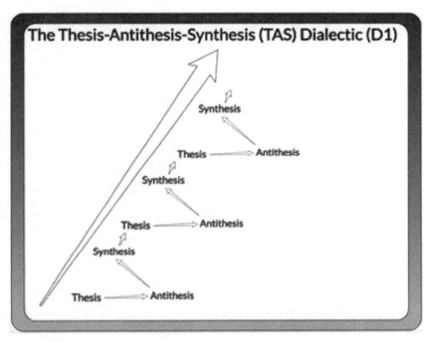

Figure 3.3   Rendition of Arendt's zigzag of dialectical movements

Arendt's work combines the revised spiraling theorization with aspects of a second dialectic, the '*negation of the negation*'. Hannah Arendt's (1978: 49) drawing we have rendered as: (1) Zigzag dialectic of progress, and (2) Will's Power of Negation (Not-Being, Not-Becoming). This is Arendt's revival of Hegel in recent decades. The first kind of dialectic is the zigzag:

> The ingenuity of the triadic dialectical movement – from Thesis to Antithesis to Synthesis – is especially impressive when applied to the modern notion of Progress ... cycle of Becoming ... Although the original movement is by no means progressive but swings back and returns upon itself, the motion from Thesis to Thesis establishes itself behind these cycles and constitutes a rectilinear line of progress. (Arendt 1978: 49)

The second kind of dialectic is the Negation, giving Future primacy over present and past (Arendt is citing Hegel's *Science of Logic*, p. 118 in the first excerpt and Nietzsche in the second):

> Being and Nothingness 'are the same thing, namely Becoming ... One direction is Passing Away'. Being passes over into Nothing; but equally Nothing is its own opposite, a transition to Being, that is Arising. (Arendt 1978: 50)

> the willing ego's time concept and the primacy it gives the future over the present and the past. The Will, untamed by Reason and its need to think, negates the present (and the past) even when the present confronts it with the actualization of its own project ... Left to itself, man's Will 'would rather will Nothingness than not will'. (Arendt 1978: 50)

In other words, the two kinds of dialectics (*thesis-antithesis-synthesis* zigzag) and the Negation (of the Negation) constitute a zigzag movement of progressing force and annihilating force.

> The dialectical process itself *starts* from Being, takes Being for granted (in contradistinction to a *Creatio ex nihilo*) in its march toward Not-Being and Becoming. The initial Being lends all further transitions their reality, their existential character, and prevents them from falling into the abyss of Not-Being. (Arendt 1978: 50, italics added)

In Depth: Hegel's 'Negation of the Negation' as an Example of Narrative-Counternarrative Dialectics

Many stop at *thesis-antithesis-synthesis* and have no idea of the Hegelian 'negation of the negation' dialectical movement. Heidegger (1927/1962) moves away from a 'negation of the negation' dialectical method and develops a different approach to time in his classic book, *Being and Time*. Heidegger's move is to change the negation of the negation dialectic Hegel deploys, to allow space its own 'multiplicity of points' and not be subordinated to what Hegel calls 'punctuality' (Heidegger 1927/1962: #430). As you know, Marx objected to Hegel having a spirituality force involved in the dialectic. Heidegger's (2003, *Four Seminars* between 1966 and 1973) develops insights into Marx's dialectic, and explores the implications of quantum physics since his (1927/1962) *Being and Time* book. We can see the role of Etiology in Heidegger's amendment to the Hegelian notion of the negation of the negation kind of dialectic. In every change the system of organization has to overcome itself, in an 'unending battle against itself' (Heidegger 1927/1962: #434). The negation of the negation in 'dialectic-Becoming' is a process of system change (and movement). Slavoj Žižek (2012), Sartre (1960/2004), and Judith Butler (2004; 2005), by contrast, reclaim Hegel's '*negation of the negation*' dialectic method by linking it up with Jacques Lacan's dialectic approach to psycho-analysis. Then, going back to Heidegger, the spatializing of Heres, the tem-poralizing of Times of Nows, and the movement in its history of experiences puts negation of the negation into relationality with qualitative-multiplicity of movement.

> It is clear that the dialectic of sense-certainty is nothing else but the simple history of its movement or its experience, and sense-certainty itself is nothing else but just this history. (Heidegger 1927/1962: 109)

There is a multiplicity approach to 'negation of the negation' which Žižek is contributing.

> In order to be One, one has to be multiple (to participate in multiplicity), and so on – 'everything would fall apart, and great havoc would follow, if it turned out that there could be a contradiction in the order of forms themselves' – 'if someone could show that kinds and forms themselves have in themselves these opposite properties, that would call for astonishment. But if someone should demonstrate that I am one thing and many, what's astonishing about that?'. (Žižek 2012: 51)

> There is multiplicity because the One is in itself barred, out-of-joint with regard to itself: This brings us on to another consequence of this weird ontology of the thwarted (or barred). One: the two aspects of a parallax gap (wave and particle, say) are never symmetrical, for the primordial gap is between (curtailed) something and nothing, and the complementarity between the two aspects of the gap function so that we have first the gap between nothing (void) and something, and only then, in a (logically) second time, a second 'something' that fills in the Void, so that we get a parallax gap between two somethings. (Žižek 2012: 928)

LIVING STORY DIALOGISMS

A 'Living Story' is compatible with an IWOK. IWOK-'living story' has a place, a time, and a mind all its own (TwoTrees 1997; 2000; TwoTrees and Kolan 2016; Boje 2001). The idea that a living story has a mind is foreign to WWOK, but natural to IWOK. Living Story is also in space, in time, and in mattering, appearing differently in WWOK and IWOK. Living Story also demonstrates the importance of Time and Place/Space as agential characters in the story, whether explicitly or implicitly. Living Story tends to be fragmented, dynamic, and in flux.

Living Story is especially suited to research addressing quantumness, complexity, and dynamic systems. Living Story for us is like Wil McWhinney's metaphor of a different type baseball. This type of baseball game is the same as American baseball, except that when the ball is in the air, the other team can move the bases.

ENSEMBLE LEADERSHIP THEORY WITH ENSEMBLE STORYTELLING

Ensemble Leadership Theory (Rosile, Boje, and Claw 2018) asserts that Ensemble leaders engage in storytelling differently. Ensemble Leadership is about collaborative 'together-telling' rather than top-down power-over telling. It is an IWOK theory of how 'everyone is a leader' in ways of 'together-telling'. It is an alternative to the managed storytelling found in storytelling organizations that are hierarchical and centralized, with the people at the top controlling who gets to do the telling. Ensemble Storytelling also relates to Living Story. A living story is dialogical, not dialectical, because it is about 'together-telling'. Further, due to its affinity with IWOK and Living Story, Ensemble Storytelling tends to incorporate features of sociomateriality, political economy, and sharing of storytelling roles and authorship (Rosile et al. 2020 forthcoming).

The case example of the Coalition of Immokalee Workers (the CIW) offers many examples of Ensemble Leadership Theory as enacted with Ensemble Storytelling. When the CIW put on an educational play (a skit) as part of their demonstration and educational weekend in Columbus, Ohio, they used several Ensemble processes. First, the actors were also the 'stage hands' who carried the parts of the simple set from the truck to the stage. During the performance, members of the audience were invited to participate on stage. At various stages of the performance, audience members were asked 'What do you see?'.

In contrast to Boje's view that the term 'storytelling' is the broadest term in this field with 'narrative' being a sub-set, Gabriel uses different definitions. It is important for the researcher choosing their theory to be clear about which storytelling definition and which storytelling theoretical approach they wish to employ.

Stories are narratives with plots and characters, generating emotion in narrator and audience, through a poetic elaboration of symbolic material. (Gabriel 2000: 5, italics in original)

I shall argue not all narratives are stories; in particular, factual or descriptive accounts of events that aspire at objectivity rather than emotional effect must *not* be treated as stories. (Gabriel 2000: 5, italics added)

However, the mythologized past that is celebrated in organizational nostalgia is 'generally idealized' and bears little relation to 'documented history'. (Gabriel 2000: 170–7, as cited in Clark and Rowlinson 2002: 11)

NARRATIVE RETROSPECTIVE SENSEMAKING THEORY

Karl Weick (1995: 128) defines narrative retrospective sensemaking as: 'typically searching for a causal chain', 'the plot follows – either the sequence beginning-middle-end or the sequence situation-transformation-situation. But sequence is the source of sense.' Barbara Czarniawska (1998: 78) says narrative: 'consists of a plot comprising causally related episodes that culminate in a solution to a problem'. These definitions are rooted in Aristotle (350 BCE 1450b: line 25 p. 233), who defines narrative as 'imitation of an action that is complete in itself, as a whole of some magnitude ... Now a whole is that which has beginning, middle, and end.' Applying Barthes petrification of narrative thesis, where 'every narrative becomes new with each retelling, and the "petrification" of stories is not the result of the myopia of the researcher but of intense stabilizing work by the narrators' in organizations' (Czarniawska 2004: 38).

ANTENARRATIVE PROSPECTIVE SENSEMAKING

Boje (2001: 10–11) developed eight renditions of antenarrative. The initial definition was about 'ante' having two meanings 'before-narrative' (and before-story) and 'bets on the future'. Antenarrative is defined as constitutive prospective sensemaking processes of both story and narrative. Over the years, these two original meanings (the before, and the 'bets on the future') were joined by other B-Concepts: the beneath, between, and the becoming of antenarrative processes in a sociomateriality notion of storytelling (Rosile et al. 2013).

Antenarrative is anticipated in Friedrich Nietzsche's (1968) *The Will to Power*. Nietzsche's Preface relates his antenarrative: 'The history of the next two centuries', 'describe what is coming, what can no longer come differently: *the advent of nihilism*', 'the future speaks now in a hundred signs, this destiny announces itself everywhere' (p. 3). In order to better understand antenarrative, we look to Boje's definition of storytelling. At the heart of the storytelling paradigm are these *six antenarrative processes* which for ease of memory, we call the *six Bs*: *before, beneath, beyond, between, becoming,* and *bets on the future* (see Figure 3.4).

In Depth: Boje's Detailed Theory Answer to the Question 'What Is Storytelling?'

Storytelling is defined as the interplay and entanglement of five forces of *intersubjectivity* (listed below):

Note: intersubjectivity refers to the ways in which the phrase 'you know' suggests how most of the storytelling is untold, unwritten, unarticulated, yet is there as a shared understanding between communicators (Boje 1991).

1. The first force, the narrative-counternarrative dialectic (*thesis-antithesis-synthesis*) tends towards *Abstracting* in the idealism of Grand Narratives like Marxism, the linguistic turn, and Western narratology of WWOK. We notice that WWOK has changed little since Aristotle's (350 BCE) *narrative poetics* (Boje 2001).
2. The second force, the living story webwork, tends towards *Grounding* in *Indigenous Ways of Knowing* (Rosile 2016), in the TamaraLand (Boje 1995) of any organization, and in Mikhail Bakhtin's (1981) *dialogisms* (polyphonic, stylistic, chronotopic, and architectonic of multiple discourses' interanimation) (Boje 2008). Some of these are in the terrestrial vibrant mattering (Bennett 2008; 2010) of *spacetimemattering* (Barad 2007).
3. The third force is another kind of dialectic (*negation of the negation*) tending towards the *Futuring* of 'prospective sensemaking' (Boje 1991; 1995; 2008).
4. This futuring is resounding in 'retrospective sensemaking' (Weick 1995) by the *rehistoricizing* of *diffracting* multiple histories (some that never were), and selecting histories that matter to projects in the present.
5. The fifth and final force is pre-constitutive of the abstracting, grounding, futuring, and rehistoricizing. This fifth force we call the *antenarrating processes* of the Bs*: before, beneath, bets on the future, becoming, between, and beyond* (Boje 2001; 2008; 2011a; Svane 2018; Boje, Svane, and Gergerich 2016).

Antenarrative theory's six main pre-constitutive processes can be arrayed on a vertical axis (beneath, beyond, and between) and a horizontal axis (before, bets, and becoming) (see Figures 3.4 and 3.5).

We are indebted to Marita Svane (2019), for her work in antenarrative, in particular, work on the *beyond, the foregrasping,* the 6th B (Boje 2014; 2019b). The ethic of forecaring includes forehaving, forestructuring, foreconcepting, foregrasping and bets on the future (all made in advance, preparing for this future rather than other futures to arrive). 'Hermeneutic storytelling means a method of research interpreting the storytelling by "critical" questioning and

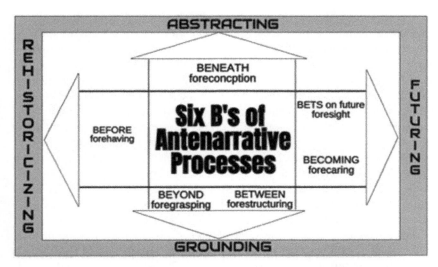

Figure 3.4   Antenarrative theory of abstracting, grounding, futuring, and rehistoricizing

investigating the facticity of the multiplicity of the storytelling and the habits of care' (Boje 2019b: 127). Boje and Svane have situated antenarrative processes in relation to Heidegger (1923/1988/1999; 1927/1962) (fore) concepts.

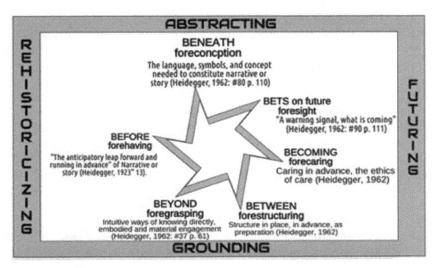

Figure 3.5   Antenarrative theory 6 Bs with Heidegger sources

It is time for antenarrating to do more '*Grounding*' than '*Abstracting*' and more '*Futuring*' than '*Rehistoricizing*' to create a paradigm shift in 'storytelling science'. WWOK narratives have been obsessed with 'abstracting', that is, reducing lived experiences to simplistic, linear plots that are inadequate to 'Indigenous Ways of Being' (IWOB), and IWOK by storytelling (Rosile 2016). We must emphasize that a 'living story web' in IWOB/IWOK is not the same as narrative-counternarrative in narratology. WWOK narratology has been all about linking some few events into linear-plot-form instead of *grounding* in the substance of the ontology of existence. Narratology has been obsessed with retrospective narrative sensemaking (rehistoricizing the past) rather than the work of Futuring by prospective sensemaking about *futuring* (Boje 2001; 2008; 2011a; 2014; 2019b). Karl Weick (2011) recognized the value of antenarrating, of prospective sensemaking in its relation to his pioneering work on retrospective narrative sensemaking.

'We no longer have recourse to the grand narratives – we can resort neither to the dialectic of Spirit nor even the emancipation of humanity as a validation for postmodern scientific discourse' (Lyotard 1979/1984: 60; see also Boje and Dennehy 1993; Boje, Gephart, and Thatchenkery 1996). Our book introduces you to 'little s' '*storytelling science*' paradigm shifts in theory-method-*praxis*. We offer ways to do theory, method, and *praxis*, in the context of the '***onto-logical turn***' (away from the 'linguistic turn') to what we call '***ensembles of multiplicities***' rooted in the works of Gilles Deleuze and Jean Paul Sartre, both trying to amend Henri Bergson's pioneering work on multiplicities.

Ensembles of 'little stories' are dialogic, and many times dialectic to 'Big Stories' and 'Grand Narratives' as ensembles of multiplicity fracture and coalesce, absorb, and interpenetrate. Sartre's (1960/2004) theory of *practical ensembles of multiplicities*, is similar to Deleuze's (1994: 240–1) intensive multiplicity of *spatium* (or 'intensive space … a pure energy') in 'the theater of all metamorphosis or difference in itself which envelops all its degrees in the production of each'. In Deleuze, there are three (3) multiplicities (extensive, intensive, and virtual). Of these three, the extensive multiplicity and the intensive multiplicity have a 'virtual object' of multiplicity at their centers. Elsewhere in this book you will find further discussion of multiplicities.

Walter Benjamin (1928/2016), for us, has done the most pioneering work in antenarrative. His book, *One Way Street*, contains 60 vignettes. Each is about the signs and symbols of a German city, following the destruction of World War I. Our antenarrative reading is Benjamin looking at the wreckage of history, trying to make sense of 'what's next', 'what future is arriving'. As yet there is no narrative or counternarrative, only fragments, clues as to which of many futures will befall humanity. He is in Germany following WWI, trying to sort out a foresight into the future of modernity. He does this by being a flâneur (stroller) through the city, and notebooking some 60 signals, signs, and intuitive insights. These have no particular theme or plot. Yet, together they are a kind of foresight, and what is called 'prospective sensemaking'.

Next we consider the four (4) Waves of Grounded Theory. We explain why David feels this method is too often invoked to cover weaknesses in both ground and in theory. We offer 4th Wave Grounded Theory as an answer to such weaknesses.

WHAT DOES IT MEAN FOR THEORY TO BE GROUNDLESS?

Most so-called *Grounded Theory* dissertations have not asked the question, *which wave of Grounded Theory is being done?* When all is said and done, Grounded Theory tries to inquire into the 'insolvable residuum a content of phenomena' that will not be explained by *spacetimecausality* or *sufficient reason* even by multiple rounds of logical positivism coding of themes and subthemes, since there is 'this unfathomable something' in the 'nature of existence' and its Being, the *'qualitates occultae'* that is 'unfathomable because it is without ground' (Schopenhauer 1928: 90–2). Without attempts of Grounded Theory to refute and disconfirm a specific paradigm by self-correcting induction, the false, the self-deceitful, the crude induction, and the perfidious, may appear more valid, that is warranted, when there is only the affirmed or the confirmed without tests of refutation or disconfirmation. Without refutation or a self-correcting type of process, early waves of Grounded Theory risk appearing a fraudulent science, or worse a pseudo-science.

In the context of pure materialism, pure 'Big Science', pure 'Big Theory', and pure 'Logic', knowledge is groundless in the Kantian *a priori* sense. (Schopenhauer 1928: 87). Immanuel Kant (1889) defined space and time as *a priori* to sensemaking, as antecedent concepts necessary to consciousness. Space and time are all, for Kant, just ideas, and they have a relation or connection to some other ideas. These ideas may be viewed as groundless schemata, in what Karl Popper (1994) called *'The Myth of the Framework'* and what Schopenhauer called the *morphology*. This is what, in Grounded Theory, is the theme and sub-theme analysis after rounds of semi-structured interviews or ethnographic case studies. These interviews and cases may be done in meticulous etiology but without co-inquiry, lacking any historical depth, and without much refutation. Such research can become just bombastic (high-sounding writing and speech acts) idea stacked upon idea without, as Heidegger (1927/1962) puts it, actually **'Being-in-the-world'** *in space, in time, in mattering,* or in the inseparability of *spacetimemattering*.

Does something remain unfathomable, the 'untold story' (Hitchin 2015), or is it the enchantment that is unfathomable to sufficient reason, that evades logic, and is something more than pure materialism or even the sociomaterialism of *spacetimemattering*? In *Quantum Storytelling*, there is no complete and finished storytelling etiological historical account, no matter its ethnographic meticulousness, or morphology of thematic typology-building, no matter the logical positivism applied. Each case in its place, in time, and in mattering, and in the inseparability of *spacetimemattering*, does not penetrate the extensiveness multiplicities of the 'inner nature of things' that comprise the forces of nature and 'that which is without ground' (Schopenhauer 1928: 87).

Therefore, when we say *Grounded Theory* has *no ground* and *no theory*, we mean several insights. First, unless the morphology search for typologies and/or the etiology case comparisons have tests, refutation, and falsification steps, then it is impossible to claim either *ground* or *theory* that is pure or even empirical science. Second, to be *grounded* and to be *theory*, there needs to be more than *post hoc* accumulation by snowball sampling, and *after-the-fact* cherry-picking of inductive inference after more and more inductive inference.

A third reason for questioning the ground of Grounded Theory is that the potentiality of *Grounded Theory* needs to have some kind of methodology of *self-correcting induction*. This book will explain self-correcting induction to you, as a way of learning by reasoning in advance of each round of inquiry, by performing disconfirmation of what Karl Popper calls *conjectures*. The researcher must do what Charles Sanders Peirce calls *self-correcting* induction that brings an inquirer who is *fallible*, doing either *quantitative induction* or *qualitative induction* or their *combination,* to something beyond mere *crude induction* that now often passes muster as so-called *Grounded Theory*.

Finally, most so-called *Grounded Theory* dissertations have not asked the question, *which wave of Grounded Theory is being done?* When all is said and done, Grounded Theory tries to inquire into the 'insolvable residuum a content of phenomena' *(sic.)* that will not be explained by *spacetimecausality* or *sufficient reason* even by multiple rounds of logical positivistic coding of themes and subthemes, since there is 'this unfathomable something' in the 'nature of existence' and its Being, the *'qualitates occultae'* that is 'unfathomable because it is without ground (Schopenhauer 1928: 90–2).

Even a logical positivist such as Carnap did not theorize logical positivism as foundationalism-epistemology, which he absolutely rejected (Friedman 1991: 508). Rather for Carnap, it is like that classic fable of the blind philosopher-scientists making sense of the parts of the elephant, unable to fathom the whole outside the *logicism* of each's own foundational paradigm. Truth depends on the choice of which science philosophy, which *logicism,* is being selected by which paradigm inquirer.

In the elephant example, the sensemaking scientist immediately chooses the logicism of the five senses and direct experience (except for sight since the hypothetical scientists are blind) for its logical empiricism of the nimble trunk. Linguists such as Wittgenstein choose the logicism of language games of the elephant's floppy ears. Sociomaterialist logicism feels the elephant tail with observer effect, it wiggles and becomes collapsed from particles into the wave effect. A logical positivist scientist notices the different curvature of the tusks and says it is the intermediary between Kantian *a priori* and traditional naïve empiricism (this, of course, is Carnap himself in this analogy). The mathematician scientist notices the number of elephant feet is the square root of four, thus this is the logicism of choice. The naturalism scientist smells the elephant dung and is amazed by the logicism of naturalism. The Euclidean geometry scientist is arguing with the Gödel geometry logicism scientist and they just cannot agree on the sex of the elephant.

Friedman's (1991: 510) point is that logical positivists get a bad rap, because most of the Vienna Circle were not epistemological-foundationalists. Further, they had this anomaly called Relativity Theory to fathom, which was shaking up Kantian *a priori*, Euclidian geometry, and in later years, the Copenhagen Interpretation of the double slit experiment, which shook the foundation of Newtonian physics:

> The first point to notice is that the positivists' main philosophical concerns did not arise within the context of the empiricist philosophical tradition at all. The initial impetus for their philosophizing came rather from late nineteenth-century work on the foundations of geometry by Riemann, Helmholtz, Lie, Klein, and Hilbert – work which, for the early positivists, achieved its culmination in Einstein's theory of relativity. (Friedman 1991: 510)

In sum, without attempts of Grounded Theory to refute and disconfirm a specific paradigm by self-correcting induction, we risk obtaining the false, the self-deceitful, the crude induction, and the perfidious. When there is only the affirmed, only that which is confirmed without tests of refutation or disconfirmation, then early waves of Grounded Theory are susceptible to appearing as a fraudulent science, or worse a pseudo-science. This is the problem of the twenty-first century: how can the heart of care up-spiral above the down spiral of the *nihilism* of what Karl Popper (1956/1983: 304) calls the 'inductive gambler'.

There are three kinds of induction in waves of Grounded Theory. 'Crude Induction' is most of early (1st Wave) Grounded Theory. 'Quantitative Induction' is in its 2nd Wave. Then there is 'Qualitative Induction' in the 3rd Wave Grounded Theory. In the 4th Wave Grounded Theory, the 'Qualitative Induction' is existential (Boje 2019b), and that is the type which we would like to share with you (see Figure 3.6).

In the 1st Wave Grounded Theory, the ground problem is with ethics and the storyteller's way of knowing since it is all about disembodied ideas. It is a Crude approach to Induction (see all eight volumes of Pierce's collected papers). We placed 1st Wave Grounded Theory on what Charles Sanders

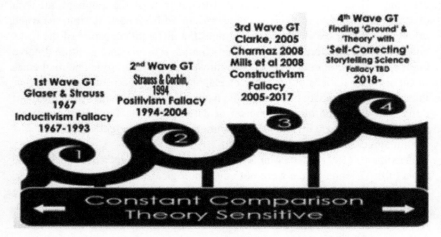

Figure 3.6   Annotated four Waves of Grounded Theory

Peirce terms the 'crude induction' side of the storytelling paradigm, and away from quantitative and qualitative induction (refer again to Figures 3.1 and 3.2). Glaser and Strauss (1967) offer a method of constant comparison of qualitative 'data' with code-categories. Here, the relationships to the objective world are external to the mind of the teller, and determined by the subject's telling of Ideas. Glaser and Strauss focus on 'open coding' the data line by line (or word by word) by attaching codes to fragments of text, not unlike how NVivo coding is done by highlighting texts and assigning codes. Holton (2008: 42) gives an account of the breakup of Barry Glaser and Anselm Strauss and how 1st Wave Grounded Theory continued on in Glaser's work and among his colleagues to this day:

> The well documented schism in the collaboration between Glaser and Strauss occurred with the publication of Basics of Qualitative Research (Strauss and Corbin 1990). Glaser's (1992) response was Basics of Grounded Theory: Emergence vs. Forcing in which he set out to distinguish the original methodology from Strauss and Corbin's work which he clearly regarded as a remodeled method that he has termed 'full conceptual description' (p.123). His continuing concern with the eroding impact of various subsequent 'remodelings' of the original methodology has motivated him to produce several additional publications in which he endeavors to clarify the purpose, principles and procedures that together constitute classic, or Glaserian, Grounded Theory (Glaser 2001; 2002; 2003; 2004; 2005; 2007; 2008; Glaser and Holton 2004). This collection of works, a result of his dedication to advancing the original methodology, offers researchers a solid base for its study and application.

The 2nd Wave Grounded Theory (Strauss and Corbin 1990; 1994/1998; Corbin and Strauss 2007) tries to compensate by turning to empirical coding of the theme-forms into categories (typologies) using (post) positivism. Glaser (1992) accuses Strauss and new partner Corbin of moving away from the emergence method, and forcing categories on the data, in a return to data verification and interpretivism. Defenders of 2nd Wave Grounded Theory (Kelle 2007) argue that Glaser does protest too much, and the empirical axial coding (defined as coding between categories' and subcategories' particular properties and dimensions) is not forcing anything. These 2nd Wave defenders then give the countercharge that Glaser (1992) in his polemic style of writing is ignoring the literature of theory in order not to contaminate his (Glaser's) standpoint on emergence.

Seidel and Urquhart (2013) side against Glaser, pointing out that there is no empirical evidence that the 2nd Wave Grounded Theory is forced coding. Seidel and Urquhart (2013: 239) accuse Glaser of 'positivism' and contend that Strauss and Corbin are from the 'American pragmatist' paradigm of Mead and Dewey, and add: 'Glaser ... requested the 1990 book to be withdrawn, arguing that Strauss' understanding of grounded theory "misconceives our conceptions of grounded theory to an extreme degree, even destructive degree" (Glaser 1992: 1)'.

The 3rd Wave Grounded Theory swings back into 'social constructivism' (internal mind of beholders), but (reluctantly? or habitually?) keeps vestiges of (post) positivism with endless thematic-coding for publication purposes. The 3rd Wave Grounded Theory (or 'constructivist Grounded Theory') departs from 1st Wave and 2nd Wave Grounded Theory by claiming that both theories and date are not discovered, but are constructed by the researcher in their inter-actions with the field of scholarship. Some 3rd Wave Grounded Theory (e.g. Charmaz 2006: 16) backs off commitment to axial coding since it 'may extend or limit your vision, depending on your subject matter and ability to tolerate ambiguity'. Charmaz (2006: 165) includes two quite brief mentions of 'abduc-tion' (from American Pragmatist Peirce) as part of the social constructivism methodology. Suddaby (2006: 638, as cited in Seidel and Urquhart 2013: 240) concurs, pointing out 'the act of research has a creative component that cannot be delegated to an algorithm'. Suddaby provides a definition of abduction, without its Peircean triadic partners of deduction and induction:

Abduction (is) a type of reasoning that begins by examining data and after scrutiny of these data, entertains all possible explanations for the observed data, and then forms hypotheses to confirm or disconfirm until the research arrives at the most plausible interpretation of the observed data. (Suddaby 2006: 638)

Abduction is mentioned only twice in the entire book, once as the definition given above, and in one other place (p. 185). Charmaz (2006) seems to confuse abductive-hypotheses with actual tests to confirm or disconfirm a theory, whether by deductive challenges of links of premises to conclusions, or by induction of cases to a population. Including the abduction definition, disconfirm has only one mention, and confirm has seven mentions (in addition to the above definition). Reading the book, there is not much there in 3rd Wave Grounded Theory about disconfirming, and what is there is seeking to confirm.

1. 'Beliefs in a unitary method of systematic observation, replicable experiments, operational definitions of concepts and logically deduced hypotheses, confirmed evidence – often taken as the scientific method – formed the assumptions' (p. 4).
2. 'Dalton received confidential documents confirming the status characteristics of managers from a secretary who believed in the value of Dalton's project' (p. 41).
3. 'Although member-checking generally refers to taking ideas back to research participants for their confirmation, you can use return visits to elaborate your categories' (p. 111).
4. 'He gained confirmation of his view then pushed further later in the same conversation' (p.112).
5. Page 132 is about confirming emergent ideas but as she says 'does not equal verification' by 'systematic quantitative procedures' (p.132).
6. 'Checking hunches on confirming ideas, in my view, does not equal verification. Rather than contributing verified knowledge, I see grounded theorists as offering plausible accounts' (p. 149).

There are four (4) Peircean disconfirmation tests which we review in Chapter 2. These four (4) are the basis of self-correcting induction methodology, and are the basis of 4th Wave Grounded Theory. For Popper, refutation of one's own theory is done by acts of falsifiability, seeking to disconfirm, not just to confirm. The 3rd Wave Grounded Theory method suggesting the researcher 'be willing to experiment with different arrangements of your memos' and to 'play with them' is not a disconfirmation experiment (Charmaz 2006: 117). It is the logical positivism mix of 3rd Wave social constructivism, with the method of 2nd Wave Grounded Theory's logical positivism. *Abduction-hypotheses need not only to be confirmed, but also actively disconfirmed for a storytelling science, be it Western Science or Native Science, to be part of the growth of scientific knowledge.*

As 'anomalies' arise, 'pockets of disorder' and the needs for refinement: of concepts, theories, observation apparatus, and practice experiments are undertaken in acts of what we are calling after Peirce (and to some extent Popper) 'self-correcting induction' tests, falsifications, and refutations. The anomalies we raise with 1st, 2nd, and 3rd Wave Grounded Theory are that there is confirmation without disconfirmation. That situation does not help either 'little s' 'storytelling science' or its interplay with 'Big S' 'Big Storytelling' evolution or revolution.

The 4th Wave Grounded Theory is a revolt, the ontological turn, and a return to IWOK ontology of Being-in-the-world, embodied and entangled in the inseparability of Quantum Storytelling of *spacetimemattering*. IWOK ontology is about becoming, the becoming of mattering, the cause and effect explanation in nature by Being-in-Nature in *spacetimemattering with spirituality*. Meanwhile the Baradians prefer no spirituality, but a posthumanist ethical standpoint to be one up on humanism. What does refutation mean for 4th Wave Grounded Theory? Answer: it means what Karl Popper (1963) calls having *refutations* for our *conjectures* rather than just doing *confirmations* of some theory propositions or framework (Popper 1994).

In sum, 1st, 2nd, and 3rd Wave Grounded Theory lack self-correction, are not doing tests of refutation, and are only loading up confirming observations. It is the ultimate 'crude' induction fallacy. It is time we tried Peirce's method of self-correcting induction, not the crude form, but the quantitative and/or qualitative mode. Peirce allows us to get to deduction from premises and/ or abductive propositions by sampling and doing inductive inquiry, as the basis for storytelling research methodology. A deduction from Grounded Theory that is ideal cannot just be studied by cherry-picking experiences of self and others, *post hoc* (after-the-fact). This is a point that 1st, 2nd, and 3rd Wave Grounded Theory has completely missed. Peirce (1931/1960: 2.729, pp. 455–6, boldness ours) adds, '**Nor must we lose sight of the constant tendency of the inductive process to correct itself**. This is of its essence. This is the marvel of it.' This self-correcting process is the basis of 4th Wave Grounded Theory (Boje 2019b) by leading to closer approximations to the 'true' by the triadic of abduction-induction-deduction.

We hope you do not choose just the 1st Wave Grounded Theory crude induction, and not a 2nd Wave Grounded Theory which is closer to Peirce's 'quantitative induction' 'inference-making'. We hope that not even the 3rd Wave Grounded Theory, with aspects of qualitative induction, is good enough for you. We hope you hold out for 4th Wave Grounded Theory. There you will find the storytelling of ontologic existence and articulated storytelling of the 'untold story' (Hitchin 2015); the *spacetimemattering* of 'storytelling organizations' (Boje 1991; 1995; 2008); the Qualimetrics multi-method interplay of qualitative, quantitative, and financial aspects; or the critical accounts and Ethnostatistics, which we will discuss in the next chapter.

4. Storytelling paradigm method, including types of induction, narrative retrospective, antenarrative prospective, integrative qualitative-quantitative methods, narrative inquiry, and multiplicities

We return again to the storytelling paradigm model already presented, and repeated here as Figure 4.1. We have already discussed the 'Theory' portion of

STORYTELLING PARADIGM	WESTERN WAYS OF KNOWING **WWOK**			INDIGENOUS WAYS OF KNOWING **IWOK**	
THEORY	Quantum Storytelling Theory				
	Narrative Retrospective Sensemaking	Narrative-Counternarrative Dialectics		Living Story Dialogisms	
				Ensemble Leadership Theory	
	Antenarrative Prospective Sensemaking				
	2nd Wave Grounded Theory	3rd Wave Grounded Theory	4th Wave Grounded Theory	1st Wave Grounded Theory	
METHOD	Self-Correcting Induction Method			Crude Induction	
	Quantitative Induction	Qualitative Induction			
	Narrative Quantification	Ethno-statistics	Qualimetrics	Critical Accounting	
PRAXES	Storytelling Multiplicities Analyses				
	Socio-Economic Storytelling			Critical Accounts	Appreciative Inquiry
	Text-based Restorying	Embodied Restorying Process			
	True Storytelling				

Figure 4.1   Storytelling paradigm theory, method, and praxis

this figure, and we move now to the 'Method' portion. Following this, Chapter 5 will address '*praxis*'.

WHAT METHODS OF INDUCTION WILL YOU CHOOSE: CRUDE, QUANTITATIVE, QUALITATIVE, SELF-CORRECTING?

Next we discuss further the meaning of 'self-correcting induction' and the forms of induction (crude, quantitative, or qualitative) you choose for your research method (seen in Figure 4.2). We offer a detailed example of a New Zealand dissertation by Mark van der Klei, using self-correcting induction. After this example, we explore various philosophers' views on self-correcting inductions. Then we offer approaches which combine qualitative and quantitative methods (shown in Figure 4.2), including Ethnostatistics, Qualimetrics, and critical accounting. We conclude this with a presentation of several kinds of storytelling multiplicities.

STORYTELLING PARADIGM	WESTERN WAYS OF KNOWING WWOK				INDIGENOUS WAYS OF KNOWING IWOK
METHOD	Self-Correcting Induction Method				
	Qualitative Induction	Quantitative Induction			Crude Induction
	Narrative Inquiry	Ethno-statistics	Qualimetrics	Critical Accounting	
	Storytelling Multiplicities Analyses				

Figure 4.2   What methods will you choose?

Before we get into the famous philosophers' views on self-correcting induction, it may be helpful to have a novice-level understanding of this (if you have not already developed this yourself). In very simple terms, self-correcting means to begin with an indirect approach, use a conversational style that encourages feedback, then reflect on the feedback to inform and adjust the inquiry as needed. An even simpler description would be David's: do a little, change a little.

Next we present a detailed case example of self-correcting induction from the dissertation of Mark van der Klei, a Māori scholar at the University of Canterbury in New Zealand (see Figure 4.3). His dissertation looks at Māori people who choose information technology as a field, so van der Klei was especially interested in methods suited to 'Indigenous Ways of Knowing' (IWOK).

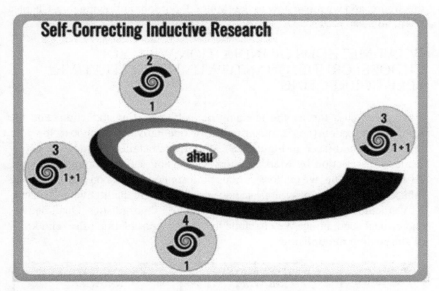

Figure 4.3   Self-correcting induction methodology (diagram by Mark van der Klei, used by permission)

Notes:
There were five rounds of conversation; each indicated by the spirals inside the circles. These double spirals symbolize a '*kōrero*' or conversational *praxis*; where the ideas and experiences of the researcher were explored and tested through interactions with participants and his supervisory team (committee). Throughout the process this involved a give-and-take approach where stories were shared between the participants and the researcher, and between the researcher and his supervisory team to ensure that everyone was an active participant or had 'skin in the game'.
Round One is '*ahau*' ('Me' or 'I' in Māori), and symbolized the auto-ethnographic approach taken by the researcher at the start of his journey. With over 10 years experience in his area of study, Mark systematically analyzed his personal experiences and examined his 'epiphany moments' against the literature and supervisory feedback to prepare his research themes.
The three streams both within and connecting each round symbolize three different intertwined activities done to ensure that learning occurred before and after each conversational storytelling back-and-forth. These were:
Analytical comparison – Constant analysis was conducted on the information gathered, be it from theory, previous recalled experiences or participant conversations.
Self-reflection – Throughout the process self-reflection was an integral part of the journey as it was used to make constant comparisons between the data gathered, Mark's role and the influence he brought to the research.
'*Tikanga*' (correct procedure, plan, or practice) – This was to ensure that what was done was done for the right reasons, and then in the right way.
The bridging lines between the three streams symbolize the central interconnecting role of self-correction in this research. Self-correction is the process of continually attempting to disprove or question any assumptions and findings that arise. The different streams had the potential to uncover different questions, and by bridging these streams constant checks were made on any questions that arose.

Round Two marked the beginning of the conversations which consisted of conversing with three information technology workers (two Māori and one non-Māori (Pākehā)). In line with autoethnography, one of the first conversations was with a previous workmate (Māori) and was done to ensure that what Mark remembered and had used as the basis of his research themes was in line with the workmate's recollection. Any differences were examined to find out the reasons, and any disproved assumptions were rejected. If this process led to new questions or theories then these were explored further in subsequent conversations.

In Round Three, five Māori IT workers were engaged in conversations – three individual one-on-one conversations and one conversation with two participants at the same time. While this was happenstance and occurred because of the organic nature of the *conversation* process, it proved to be so beneficial for this research that further conversations of this kind were sought to see if this was just a one-off experience (self-correction).

Round Four included four Māori and one non-Māori, and Round Five was five Māori with another instance of two participants being in same conversation, at the same time. While it is Mark's intention to revisit the first participants' conversations with self-corrected themes, as this has yet to be conducted this event has not been included in this model.

At our 21 March 2019 meeting at the University of Canterbury in Christchurch, New Zealand, Mark van der Klei created and presented his image of how, as a Māori scholar, he is doing self-correcting induction in his dissertation. We thank him for giving us permission to show it off to you.

Round One begins with '*ahau*' (the 'I') doing inquiry using conversational *storytelling* with himself, so he is reflecting on his own 'right way' and 'right purpose'. Before the Second round of *storytelling conversations*, this time with other folks, Mark prepares by doing his theory review and his review of Māori *praxis*. He brings a gift he made himself as a respectful way to initiate conversation. It begins with him saying who are his people, from where they hail, their relation to the land and water, and why he is there.

The conversation is back-and-forth in his first two meetings, in co-inquiry. As Mark says, 'he has skin in the game' sharing his own stories. The conversational storytelling has a purpose, but unlike semi-structured interviews, there is no list of steering questions, no linear processing of an agenda, and no interrogation-like questioning of an inquisitor. In Round Two, to engage in self-correction, Mark also does a conversation with a non-Māori (or Pākehā as they are called in New Zealand). He notices how different the conversation is and changes some of his abductive-hypotheses, and changes the manner of conversation for the next round.

Round Three is three conversations, one after the other, and a 1+1 (two people who decide to be in the conversation together). As in Round One, in Round Three Mark made his predictions, wrote them down, and after the round, made his self-corrections to his abductions and to his inductive co-inquiry conversation approach. He also reworked his deductive theory. Round Four, Mark has four more conversations with Māori folks, and one more conversation with a non-Māori (Pākehā) as a further check. At this point, Mark has completed Round Five, with three more Māori conversations, and another 1+1 conversation (two people together doing co-inquiry with Mark).

His plan at that time (March 2019) was to return to the Round Two folks and share what he has found, and get their feedback. Mark may have additional rounds after that. The point is Mark is doing self-reflexivity, setting up his theory, his abductive-hypotheses, then doing inductive inquiry conversations. He is also including tests of disconfirmation with non-Māori (Pākehā) along the way. He is interpreting the conversations and reflecting on his own role in the conversation as he does self-correcting storytelling science s/S using a cycle of abduction-induction-deduction as found in the writing of Charles Sanders Peirce. Mark van der Klei is incorporating these results in his research.

Self-correcting induction methodology can be used in *storytelling conversations*, fieldwork studies, or in conducting experiments into *praxis*, and it can be used in conducting practice changes that create new *bets on the future*. What does it mean for 4th Wave Grounded Theory? Answer: it means what Karl Popper (1963) calls having *refutations* for our *conjectures* rather than just doing *confirmations* of some theory propositions or framework (Popper 1994). In the 2019 book *Organizational Research: Storytelling in Action'* (Boje 2019b), Boje developed introductory aspects of this 'self-correcting storytelling research methodology': 'In a nutshell, self-correcting inductive method means taking a series of repeated samples from a population, each time calculating your prediction, and then verifying the results in each successive sample.' It is about developing 'fair samples' in advance rather than snow-balling them. Georg Henrik von Wright (1941/1965: 160) interprets Peirce's self-correcting induction as 'the constant tendency of induction process to correct itself' as the 'essence' and the 'marvel of induction'. Professor von Wright (1941/1965: 159, italics in original) calls it a 'self-correcting operation,' and claims it is '*the best mode of reasoning about the unknown* ... on the principle that future experience will be in conformity with the past'.

Keep in mind C. S. Peirce only wrote a few sentences about the principles and rules of a self-correcting induction-deduction-abduction method, and as yet no one in Grounded Theory or storytelling research has tried it. David has been working with doctoral students he mentors (Mabel Sanchez, Thomas Kleiner, James Sibel (2019), Anna Stevenson, Etieno Enang, Russ Barnes, and Sabrina Daddar), encouraging them to try it out in their dissertations. At the 8th annual storytelling conference (December 2018) all of us (except Etieno) got together and drew diagrams about how to do 'self-correcting storytelling methodology'. David also worked with Jens Larsen, Kenneth Mølbjerg Jørgensen, Don Pepion, Tyron Love, Duncan Pelly, Gregory Cajete, David Trafimow, Grace Ann Rosile, Manal Hamzeh, Yue Cai, Mark Hillon, Rohny Saylors, Jillian Saylors, and 40 others at the December conference to sort out this new approach to storytelling methodology using self-correcting Qualitative Induction-Abduction-Deduction.

In various amendments to business storytelling, Boje proposes to use this 'self-correcting storytelling method' to deconstruct and then transform the 'storytelling'. David applies this method to multinational water corporations and 'Water Capitalism' (Loomis 2013; Block and Nelson 2015; Saylors and Boje *in review*; Boje 2019a) to avert the impending death spiral, and instead to generate the upward spiral momentum of 'Self-Correcting Abductive-Inductive-Deductive Experiments' (Boje 2019b: 17–18, 243, and 279 in original). The good news is there are actually solutions to the world's severe water shortage, and ways to prevent 'Day Zero' when tap water ceases to flow. Water is a super wicked complexity problem, so we need to deconstruct the entire TamaraLand of the global water business if we want our grandchildren to avoid 'Day Zero' and the severe water scarcity billions of people already face. It is time for a new water future, one where all humanity has free and equal access to fresh water that is not controlled by multinational water businesses.

UNDERPINNINGS OF INDUCTION AND SELF-CORRECTING METHOD

Reading through Peirce's (1933–1937) eight volumes of collected papers, several volumes make reference to 'self-correction'. For example, Volume 5, section 576 (or 5.576) begins and ends this way: 'That Induction tends to correct itself, is obvious enough ... Broadly speaking ... we see that a properly conducted Inductive research corrects its own premises.' In self-correcting induction, the premises and/or abductive-hypotheses are written out before doing the *storytelling conversations*, observations, or experiments. In Peirce (1931–1937: 4.5): 'Induction according to ordinary logic rises from the contemplation of a sample of a class to that of the whole class' but according to the logic of relatives it rises from the contemplation of a fragment of a system to the envisagement of the complete system (Peirce 1931–1935: 6.41, 6.329, 6.473):

> 6.41 gives an example of sampling wheat to learn its latent existence '... that we are endeavoring to determine; while if, on the other hand, there is some other mode in which the wheat is to come under our knowledge, equivalent to another kind of sampling so that after all our care in stirring up the wheat some experiential grains will present themselves in the first sampling operation more often than others in the long run, this very singular fact will be sure to get discovered by the inductive method, which must

avail itself of every sort of experience; and our interference, which was only provisional, corrects itself at last'.

6.329 is about error correction The principal argument runs as follows: 'Scientific research has hitherto made plainly apparent no other cause of changes in the physical universe than brute force' and therefore it is presumable that there is no other. This is a sort of induction resting upon the principle that whatever error it may lead us into the very same argument will in time correct, if it be persisted in long enough.'

6.473 is the three types of Induction: Crude Induction of Bacon, and the two alternatives of Gradual Induction: Quantitative and Qualitative. 'The first is that which Bacon ill described ... I call this Crude Induction. It is the only Induction which concludes a logically Universal Proposition. It is the weakest of arguments, being liable to be demolished in a moment ... The other kind is Gradual Induction, which makes a new estimate of the proposition of truth in the hypothesis with every new instance; and given any degree of error there will *sometime* be an estimate (or would be, if the probation were persisted in) which will be absolutely the last to be infected with so much falsity. Gradual Induction is either qualitative or quantitative and the later depends on measurements, or on statistics, or on counting.'

There is more that Peirce theorizes about the relation of abduction (sometimes he called it retroduction) hypotheses to inductive inquiry of successive sampling, and deduction of theory to ideal circumstances. For example in Volume 7, he develops a different variant of crude induction he calls '*Rudimentary Induction*' or the 'Pooh-pooh argument proceeds from the premise that the reasoner has no evidence of the existence of any fact ... It goes by such light as we have, and that truth is bound eventually to come to light' (7.111) and is 'justified where there is no other way of reasoning' (7.113). Peirce goes on to develop a 'second order of induction' with full predictions after a hypothesis is suggested and facts observed and scrutinized, but this he calls 'Abduction' not Induction (7.114). He mentions it because many students he notices confuse Induction with Abduction, and this results in the '*post hoc ergo propter hoc* fallacy' (7.114). Popper calls it *ad hoc* hypothesizing confirming, rather than testing, refuting, and falsifying and correcting as you go. For Peirce, Induction modifies the expectation of future experience in regards to experiments or quasi-experiments. Self-correction he describes as the way 'to persist in this same method of research and we shall gradually be brought around to the truth. This gradual process of rectification is in great contrast to what takes place with rudimentary induction where the correction comes with a bang' (7.115). The Third Order Induction 'which may be called Statistical Induction, differs entirely from the other two in that it assigns a definite value to a quantity. It draws a sample of a class, finds a numerical expression for a predesignate character of that sample and extends this evaluation, under proper qualification, to the entire class, by the aid of the doctrine of chances' (7.120).

The 1st, 2nd, and 3rd Waves of Grounded Theory (discussed above, Chapter 3) lack self-correction, are not doing tests of refutation, and only are loading up confirming observations. It is the ultimate induction fallacy. It is time we tried Peirce's method of self-correcting induction, not the crude form, but the quantitative or qualitative mode of getting to deduction from premises and/ or abductive propositions by sampling and doing induction inquiry, as the basis for storytelling research methodology. By definition this '*self-correcting induction as storytelling methodology*' means arriving at a deductive general-ization by a process of successive correction to find one's way to any black swan deviant in what we initially experienced as only white swans everywhere. As von Wright (1941/1965: 160) calls it, self-correcting induction gets to deduction by 'finding one's way from the labyrinth' in a 'self-correcting oper-ation' that leads to a '*true* generalization' and some true storytelling. There is much more to this than what Professor von Wright read of Peirce's work. For example: Peirce (1931/1960: 1.95, pp. 39–40) has two rules of Induction:

1. 'The first of these is that the sample must be a random one' not a snowball.
2. 'The other rule is that the character toward the ascertainment of the proportion-ate frequency of which in the lot sampled [the sampling is done], must not be determined by the character of the particular sample taken' (bracketed addition original).

In other words, sample in advance, and do your predictions in advance, before entering the field. Then learn to challenge your conjectures with refutations, so you can be entering a learning cycle of self-correction. Sampling a few people, and refuting your theory and conjectures, learning from the errors, and then sampling a few more people, and repeating the process, is the procedure to be continued until you have eliminated all the Fake Storytelling and only the True Storytelling, if any, remains. A deduction from theory that is ideal cannot just be studied by cherry-picking experiences of self and others, *post hoc* (after-the-fact). This is a point that 1st, 2nd, and 3rd Wave Grounded Theory has completely missed. The S/s (*both* big *and* small) storytelling science we are proposing you attempt is rooted in Popper and Peirce. David found in Karl Popper's (1963: 240) book on *Conjectures and Refutations*, a reference in footnote 23 to Charles Sanders Peirce (1933–1937: 7.205–207) that gives this account of '*self-correcting induction*' (without using the phrase) and how it is different from deduction:

> #205. 'Deduction of course, relates exclusively to an ideal state of things. A hypothesis presents such an ideal state of things and asserts that it is the icon, or analogue of an experience.'
>
> #206. '... When, however, preference for putting the most unlikely ones to the test, is verified by experiment, whether without modification or with a merely quantitative modification, we begin to accord to the hypothesis a standing among scientific results. This sort of inference it is, from experiments testing predictions based on a hypothesis, that is alone properly entitled to be called *induction*.'
>
> #207. '... The critical distinction, that is, the distinction in respect to the nature of their validity between deduction and induction consists in this, – namely, deduction professes to show that certain admitted facts could not exist, even in the ideal world constructed for the purpose, either without the existence of the very fact concluded, or without the occurrence of this fact in the long run in that proportion of cases of the fulfillment of certain objective conditions in which it is concluded that it will occur ... In either case, deductive reasoning is necessary reasoning, although, in the latter case, its subject matter is probability. Induction, on the other hand, is not justified by any relation between the facts stated in the premises and the fact stated in the conclusion ... But the justification of its conclusion is that that conclusion is reached by a method which, steadily persisted in, must lead to true knowledge in the long run of cases of its application, whither to the existing world or to any imaginable world whatsoever. Deduction cannot make such a claim as this; since it does not lead to any positive knowledge at all, but only traces out the ideal consequences of hypotheses.'

Elsewhere, Peirce (1931/1960: 2.729, pp. 455–6, boldness ours) adds, '**Nor must we lose sight of the constant tendency of the inductive process to correct itself**. This is of its essence. This is the marvel of it.' This self-correcting process is the basis of 4th Wave Grounded Theory (Boje 2019b) by leading to a closer approximation to 'True Storytelling' by the triadic of abduction-induction-deduction. Thus, this method is never just one investigation, but an entire succession of investigations, drawing more and more samples, improving abductive-hypothesis and refuting theory after theory, but it is the repeated induction 'until it loses its amplicative character by the exhaustion of the class and becomes a mere deduction of that kind called *complete induction*, in which, however, some shadow of the inductive character remains, as the name implies' (Peirce 1931/1960: 2.734, p. 461). This is Peirce's as well as Popper's answer to resolving inductive fallacy that breaks his two rules.

CRUDE, QUANTITATIVE, AND QUALITATIVE INDUCTION

For Peirce, self-correcting induction is used as part of the triad of abduction-deduction-induction. We will see in Popper it is a zigzag of correcting theories and hypotheses by tests of disconfirmation, and never just confirmation.

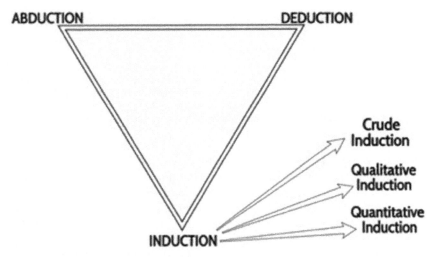

Figure 4.4   *Three types of induction in the Peircean ABDUCTION-INDUCTION-DEDUCTION (AID) triad*

Peirce (1931/1960: 2.758–759) (see Figure 4.4) puts three kinds of induction in relationship:

1. **Crude Induction**: 'Future experience will not be utterly at variance with all past experience.' This in storytelling is retrospective sensemaking narrative making linear plots.
2. **Quantitative Induction**: 'What is the "real probability" than an individual member of a certain experiential class, say the Ss will have a certain character, say that of being P?'
3. **Qualitative Induction**: Is intermediate between Crude and Quantitative Induction. 'Upon a collection of innumerable instances of equal evidential value of different parts it has to be estimated according to our sense of the impression they make upon us.' This we first deduce from 'abductive'

(or 'retroductive') hypothesis (terms he uses sometimes differently, other times interchangeably).

Crude Induction

If our central theme is correct, then the 'crude induction storytelling method of' business storytelling is replete with inductive fallacy, and needs to move to qualitative and quantitative induction storytelling methods.

Qualitative Induction

Peirce (1931/1960: 2.758–759) continues:

> Qualitative Induction consists in the investigator's first deducing from the retroductive hypothesis as great an evidential weight of genuine conditional predictions as he can conveniently undertake to make and to bring to the test, the condition under which he asserts them being that of the retroductive hypothesis having such degree and kind of truth as to assure their truth.

In other words, for qualitative induction, the researchers do prospective sensemaking, *antenarrating in advance* what they expect to find, *antecedent* to doing the field *storytelling conversations*, case studies, or experiments. This *'virtual* antecedence' as Peirce calls it, begins abductively with conjecture drawing upon available facts, and then designs a 'well-considered initial program for work upon the question' (Peirce 1931/1960: 2.758–759). Not all abduction-hypotheses will work out, and must be rejected, while trying to only 'admit the true prediction' that 'must *eventually* be so varied as to test every feature of the hypothesis; yet the interests of science command constant attention to economy, especially in the earlier inductive stages of research' (ibid., italics added). In other words there is so much multiplicity to consider of such variety, using qualitative induction means engaging in a self-correcting operation of making initial abductive predictions, ascertaining 'their truth or falsity' and then

> Having taken account of such subsidiary arguments as there may be, goes on to judge of the combined value of the evidence, and to decide whether the hypothesis should be regarded as proved, or as well on the way toward being proved, or as unworthy of further attention, or whether it ought to receive a definite modification in the light of the new experiments and be inductively reexamined *ab ovo*, or where finally, that while not true it probably presents some analogy to the truth, and that the results of the induction may help to suggest a better hypothesis. (ibid.)

In the self-correcting storytelling method, 'Qualitative induction approximates gradually, through in an irregular manner to the experiential truth for the long run. The antecedent probable error of it at any state is calculable as well as the probable error of that probable error' (Peirce 1931/1960: 2.770). David (Boje 2016d) will conclude in the section (below) about Coca-Cola, Pepsi, and Nestlé sustainability reporting, that their storytelling can calculate probable error and a 'discrepancy between the antecedent and *a posteriori* probable errors' which requires our storytelling research investigation (ibid.). The important point is that 'qualitative induction' by self-correction steps, 'always makes a gradual approach to the truth, though not a uniform one' (ibid.). We can help these soft drink and bottled water corporations get to 'True Storytelling'.

There is a sort of Copernican Revolution taking place in statistics, and in quantitative induction. David Trafimow (2012; 2014; 2019; Trafimow and Uhalt, *in press*) wants to replace 'null hypothesis significance testing' (NHST) and p-value significance testing (usually less than .05) with a wider consideration of the nature of the contribution submitted manuscripts usually receive; a greater tolerance of ambiguity; more of an emphasis on the thinking and execution of the study, with a decreased emphasis on the p-value of findings; replacing NHST with the *a priori* procedure. The *a priori* procedure pertains to the replication crisis that has become such a concern as of late.

The implication for qualitative induction, and for self-correcting induction, is to do antecedent abductive-hypothesis formulation rather than *post hoc* inference, known as confirmation bias (tendency for new abductions to confirm our existing theories, assumptions, and abductions). This is why we follow Peirce and Popper in recommending 'refutation' as part of the qualitative as well as quantitative methods.

We hope you do not choose just the 1st Wave Grounded Theory crude induction, nor a 2nd Wave Grounded Theory that is closer to Peirce's 'quantitative induction' 'inference-making', and not even the 3rd Wave Grounded Theory, which has aspects of qualitative induction. We hope you hold out for 4th Wave Grounded Theory. This includes storytelling of ontologic existence and articulated storytelling of the 'untold story' (Hitchin 2015), the *spacetimemattering* of 'storytelling organizations' (Boje 1991; 1995; 2008) and the Qualimetrics multi-method interplay of qualitative, quantitative, and financial aspects, or as we will review, the critical accounts and Ethnostatistics. Storytelling is not just qualitative, it is qualimetric. It is not just triangulation that stacks up a qualitative with a quantitative, using qualitative and quantitative in an interweaving (Boje 2018b). It is a subtle deconstruction of how people in organizations use numbers, constitute them and do storytelling about them (Gephart 1988).

Quantitative Induction

While multi-method purports to be more open to linking quantitative with qualitative methods, its so-called 'triangulation' often is not a true integration, as when it treats qualitative as a decoration for quantitative tables. This section is more about using quantitative and qualitative together, strategically, and studying how people in organizations make sense with and about numbers. Popper (2008: 59) argues in a lecture in New Zealand given in 1940, that zigzag piecemeal social experiments relying on the scientific method by an attitude of humility, fallibility, and a 'readiness to learn from mistakes' and make 'small experiments' by 'a great number of piecemeal adjustments to the various parts' of 'a great number of experiences' is preferable to the leadership of the 'megalomania tyrant' (Popper 2008: 61). Often quantitative ends up being the tyrant, subordinating qualitative, reducing it to a case illustration of a p-value.

Narrative Quantification of the Qualitative

There are books on narrative quantification (e.g. Franzosi 2010) and many software packages (NVivo, Leximancer, Dictionary, etc.) promising to do quantification of narrative texts, to save researchers the pain of actually doing their own text-analysis work. Rather than hegemonized quantification of the qualitative into a hierarchic duality, we are advocating for a more back-and-forth, self-correcting approach of equal partnering.

There is some progress. For example, 'Fussy Sets/Qualitative Case Analysis (*fs*/QCA)' by Ragin, Drass, and Davey (2006) is a fuzzy set sampling that permits membership in the interval between 0 and 1 sampling permutations of several dimensions, while retaining the two qualitative states of full membership and full non-membership in relation to traditional comparative qualitative case analysis (Drass and Ragin 1992). Studies are using *fs*/QCA with traditional quantitative 'structural equation modeling' (SEM). For example, Skarmeas, Leonidou, and Saridakis (2014) study the consumer skepticism about corporate social responsibility (CSR) in a subtle impact of CSR skepticism in contingent combinations of complex antecedent conditions and several alternative paths. What is new is *fs*/QCA, a family of methods that provides researchers with an alternative to conventional, correlational reasoning methods. 'Unlike conventional quantitative methods in social sciences, research such as systems of regression and multivariate procedures are mostly based on frequency and consistency thresholds. The basis of fuzzy set analysis is the fact that there is no "single correct answer"' (Valaei et al. 2019: 297). A multiple streams, multiple pathways approach can be used as a way to study how quantitative and qualitative are entangled together in the case example of 40 Dutch municipalities doing forward-looking decision-making about land use policies (Pot et al. 2019). Next we introduce you to some alternative methods to the usual dualistic separation of qualitative and quantitative *methods:* Qualimetrics, Critical Accounting, and Ethnostatistics.

Qualimetrics

Qualimetrics is at the heart of the Socio-Economic Approach to Management (SEAM). SEAM is the researcher-intervenor method of Savall and colleagues (Worley et al. 2015; Savall 1975/2010; Savall et al. 2018; Savall and Zardet 2008; 2011; Savall, Zardet, and Bonnet 2008). In SEAM, there are actual pre-*experiment (project)* diagnostic inquiries, hypotheses, in a scientific method. Henri Savall and Véronique Zardet (2008) situate their research paradigm between empiricist and constructivist, refusing to dualize. They invent a new term for their betwixt and between approach: '*Qualimetrics*'. Qualimetrics bridges the gap between the qualitative and the quantitative, as well as the financial methodologies.

Qualimetrics involves working in the middle between qualitative, quantitative, and financial methods. In management science, we know that the quantitative and financial has a qualitative evaluation, and vice versa. Qualimetrics is defined, then, as an intervention into the way in which numbers are produced, analyzed, displayed, and interpreted. The aim is to be more sensitive to the socio-economic context of measurement and the (dysfunctional) outcomes of how numbers are employed. Qualimetrics is this agile, adaptive approach to small experimental practices using scientific method, along with an attitude of socially responsible capitalism, all done with a spirit of cooperation in the 'socio-economic approach to management' (SEAM).

The Qualimetrics (Savall and Zardet 2008: 206) approach to bridging quantitative and qualitative follows an alternating series of deduction, induction, deduction, abduction inquiries. Qualimetrics uses a trilectical of three kinds of knowledge structuration: (1) qualitative fieldnotes and observations; (2) quantitative data about frequencies of dysfunctions; and (3) financial consequences of the hidden costs and dysfunctions not currently shown in regular accounting reports (see Boje 2011b).

Critical Accounting Research

This is a growing field with narrative methods of emancipatory accounting that negate the hegemonic effects of accounting, numbers discourse, and quantitative corporatism practices (Neu, Cooper, and Everett 2001; Jacobs 2011). Non-critical accounting typically collects and organizes financial information in economic terms for managerial purposes (Broadbent 2002). Critical Accounting is always contextual within wider critical discourse (Laughlin 1999). Laughlin (1999: 75) says Critical Accounting draws on French 'critical theorists' (such as Foucault, Derrida, Latour) and the German 'critical theorists' (such as Marx, Adorno, Habermas). Rahaman (2010), for example, looks at narratives of accounting critically, for their role in the history of colonization in Africa. Critical Accounting Methods can also be used to deconstruct narratives of neoliberalism (Chiapello 2017).

Ethnostatistics

Robert Gephart's (1988) Ethnostatistics attends to the narrative rhetoric that authors of empirical and statistical papers use to explain their numeric manipulations. Ethnostatistics has three moments. The first moment is to qualitatively question how numbers are constructed. The second moment is to analyze how the mathematical assumptions and limits of various statistical methods are being fudged or stretched. The third moment deconstructs the rhetoric of quantitative justification, and narrative articulations about statistical displays, such as using a p-value to justify a conclusion or finding. Examples of Ethnostatistics include studies of Enron's financial narratives by Smith, Gardner, and Boje (2004) and Boje, Gardner, and Smith (2006).

NARRATIVE INQUIRY METHODS

Since Aristotle, narrative inquiry has struggled to get past narrow analyses of abstract elements of narrative (plot, character, theme, dialogue, rhythm, and spectacle) to an analysis of the *whole-storytelling organization's* dynamics. The qualitative inductive analysis of storytelling organizations (Boje 1991; 1995; 2008) 'exposes a contradiction-ridden, tension-filled embattled' arena of 'dialogized heteroglossia' (Bakhtin 1981: 272). Social heteroglossia has two opposing forces, the *centripetal* centralizing socio-ideological movement and the *centrifugal* decentralization diffusion of resistance movements. For example, in a recent historical epoch, since Thatcher and Reagan, business storytelling organizations have exhibited *centripetal* centralization of neoliberalism ideology storytelling, opposed weakly by the *centrifugal* decentralization of progressivism ideology storytelling.

In Depth: Social Discourse and Bakhtinian Stylistics and Dialogisms

We are often asked to explain the relationship of social discourse to storytelling organizations. Often narrative inquiry tries to substitute narrative poetics (particularly plot and theme analysis) for the whole-storytelling dynamics of social heteroglossia. Social heteroglossia can be defined as the dialogical opposition of centripetal (centralization) forces with centrifugal (decentralization) forces of language and ideological-discourse. The linguistic turn has ignored ideological spheres of storytelling organizations. Storytelling organizations are defined as multi-voices, multi-stylistic, multi-medium, and multi-languaged, and out of this heteroglot, storytelling organization can emerge. The qualitative inductive method is a way to analyze the spheres of ideological life coursing through storytelling organizations. These spheres of ideological life in business storytelling can be analyzed using what Bakhtin (1981) calls stylistic dialogism, and its social heteroglossia of opposed centripetal (centralization) and centrifugal (decentralization) discursive life. Ideological-discourse continues to colonize storytelling organizations in six stylistic unities that act in combination (Boje 2008: 65–8; Bakhtin 1981: 262):

1. Architectural narration that tells its own material story (McStyle of McDonald's restaurant; Disneyland theme parks, etc.).
2. Direct authorial narration (every narrator's utterance, even in a qualitative inductive analysis, serves to a centripetal or centrifugal point).
3. Everyday oral narration (*skaz*, such as Nike's 'Just Do It!', or McDonald's McJob, McWork, McMeal, etc.).
4. Everyday written narration (letters, memos, email, websites, reports, diaries, corporate annual reports, corporate sustainability websites, etc.).
5. Ethnographic, scientific, and philosophical descriptive narration.
6. Individualized narration of character's dialogues (excerpts from workers, CEOs, customers, etc. inserted into an analysis).

These six ideological styles of discourse course through certain spheres of storytelling organizations. They are the stuff you repurpose in your *qualitative inductive* analyses. There is textual and verbal ideological-discourse. Social discourse has an enormous, under-researched role because the focus for decades of organization studies has been on narrative inquiry into rhetorical genres (CEO persuasion, advertising vignettes, and so on). What this does is substitute a rhetoric-part for the whole-storytelling. It reduces storytelling organization to poetic form of narrative from 'Aristotle to the present day' (Bakhtin 1981: 269). What gets ignored is the ideological life of storytelling organizations. Five dialogisms get reduced to narrative form elements analysis, rather than studying the whole-storytelling dynamic. Polyphonic dialogism (many voices), stylistic dialogism (many styles of speech and text), chronotopic dialogism (many spacetime contradictions), and architectonic dialogism (interanimations of ethical, aesthetic, and cognitive discourses). For examples see Boje and Rosile (2008), Boje, Haley, and Saylors (2016), Haley and Boje (2014). The ideological life of storytelling organizations gets reduced to this or that narrative or story vignette or to some monologic utterance by the CEO standing in for the entire social heteroglossia. Don't get us wrong: rhetoric creative persuasion in vignette-cases is important, but ought not substitute for whole-storytelling and the 'dialogized quality of discourse' (Bakhtin 1981: 269). By engaging in self-correcting qualitative-induction methods it is possible to analyze the whole life of discourse in storytelling organizations.

STORYTELLING MULTIPLICITY METHODS

Here is an example of multiplicity analysis methods from Boje (2019c) which uses Coca-Cola company reports as the basis for this case example. Coca-Cola is, in its 2017–2018 Annual Sustainability Report, for example, breaking Rule 1 (no random sampling; see Boje 2016d). The report only included selected 258 water-replenishment stories of 248 water-replenishment projects from 71 of the 200 countries in which its 250 bottling partners and 800 bottling plants operate. In actuality there are only 195 countries in the world, which means Coca-Cola is counting-challenged. And the estimated 248 billion liters (65.5 billion gallons) per year being replenished back to aquifers is a conclusion reached by Coca-Cola that seems to me to violate both induction rules of C. S. Peirce.[1] Rule 1 of inductive method necessitates a random sample of all bottlers in all countries and includes both success and failure stories. The sample pretends to be all countries.

Rule 2 would require an ***antecedent*** statement of the 'characters' (i.e. 'each story' and 'each water situation') ***before*** the sampling of replenishment cases is done for study, rather than ***post hoc*** jumping to the conclusion that all water-replenishment practices of Coca-Cola projects, worldwide, have been equally successful. The reason for Induction Rule 2 'deciding what character to examine' and 'not doing *post hoc ergo propter hoc*' inference (Peirce 1931/1960: 1.95, 1.97) is that there are three kinds of story-multiplicities and water-situation-multiplicities that need to be 'verified before any particular weight is accorded to it', and those three Deleuzian multiplicities we have been writing about, we can now apply here (Boje 2019a; 2019b):

1. **Extensive multiplicities**: Story-schema in one part of the world is different, not the same as other story-schema in another region. Deleuze (1994: 231) terms this an *extensio* form of schema. The *qualitas* forms of matter are occupying extensity. For Schopenhauer (1928) this is morphology without etiology (investigation of historical cause), more of the lived experience than the reduction to schemata; of people or water reduced to 'resources' or things or commodities, or to a privatization schema of corporate water for profit.
2. **Intensive multiplicities**: Stories have different temporal duration horizons, each with intensive force: Coca-Cola has a quarterly report time horizon; a farmer's horizon is seasonal. McDonald's has a clocktime of performativity. Water-replenishment in one kind of aquifer can take years, but in another it takes centuries or millennia.
3. **Virtual multiplicities**: Extensive and intensive are 'coextensive with virtuality' (Deleuze 1994: 193). Stories and narratives can become 'virtual objects' (p. 99) of coextensive multiplicities. Water becomes virtual, and is

in virtual use, when it is involved in production and distribution processes of a global corporate supply chain. Virtual water is hidden in what it takes to make fuel, and to erect concrete walls, and maintain a multi-million dollar bottling plant. It takes three virtual water liters to make single-use plastic or glass bottles, for every liter of water that goes into those containers.

Virtual water has consequences in the materiality of the world (Bloc 2019). To carry the example of virtual water to a deeper level of theory, we can look to Deleuze and Guattari (1994). Virtual water is not easy to think about, and can plunge us into a chaos of calculations, unable to survey our own virtual water complicity, and such is 'the reality of the virtual' (Deleuze and Guattari 1994: 210). In their critique of Badiou's theory of multiplicity, Deleuze and Guattari conclude 'the theory of multiplicities does not support the hypothesis of any multiplicity whatever (even mathematics has had enough of set-theoreticism [*ensemblisme*]). There must be at least two multiplicities, two types, from the outset. This is not because dualism is better than unity but because the multiplicity is precisely what happens between the two' (Deleuze and Guattari 1994: 152). In other words, we can begin by theorizing the possibility of 'ensembles of multiplicities', instead of a duality or monism.

The implication of their critique of Badiou for organization studies is that 'organization sets' is too simplistic a way to look at the function of organizations in relation to individuated bodies. The lived perceptions and affections that constitute opinions on everything we see, affects the 'path that descends from the virtual to states of affairs and to other actualities' (Deleuze and Guattari 1994: 155).

There is some virtual chaos involved:

> States of affairs leave the virtual chaos on conditions constituted by the limit (reference): they are actualities, even though they may not yet be bodies or even things, units, or sets. They are masses of independent variables, particles-trajectory or signs-speeds. They are *mixtures* ... This is because the state of affairs actualizes a chaotic virtuality by carrying along with it a space that has ceased, no doubt, to be virtual but that still shows its origins and serves as absolutely indispensable correlate to the state of affairs. (Deleuze and Guattari 1994: 153, italics added)

Deleuze and Guattari (1994: 153) give an example from quantum physics, which we will paraphrase. The atomic nucleus, the nucleon that is close to chaos, is also surrounded by a cloud of constantly emitted and reabsorbed particles, or the actualization of the electron in relation to a potential photon that interacts with the nucleon to give a new state of nuclear material.

Storytelling is the 'power of repetition', the 'discursive power of the function' and the 'reality of a virtual, of an incorporeal, of an impassible, in contrast with the function of an actual state, body functions, and lived function'

(p. 159). Ensembles of multiplicities are all about what happens when multiplies intersect. To use the example of 'virtual water', water is extensive across places, intensive in its timeliness, and virtual when hidden in every production and service throughout the supply chain.

We are born embodied in water, and live in that situation on a watery planet, unless the counter-effectuated event of freshwater shortages ends life. From the virtuality of water we descend to how production and consumption is actualized. The concept of virtual water gathers together the entire supply chain and acts of consumers in the cathedral of consumption. Then its 'line of actuality lays out a plane of reference that slides the chaos again: it takes from it states of affairs that, of course, also actualize virtual events in their coordinates, but it retains only potentials already in the course of being actualized, from part of the functions' (Deleuze and Guattari 1994: 160).

Virtual water gets calculated, and *praxis* is instituted based on the scientifically and legally situated state of affairs in the relation between water management and water mismanagement. The success of the virtual water revolution, its very reality, resides precisely in 'vibrations, clinches, and openings' (p. 177) Virtual water is a becoming of care, a betweenness that embodies life in 'qualitative differences' and constructs a foreseeing. It is bets on our future, of virtual possibilities of a life lived in ethical answerability for our water *praxis* in daily life, especially in work life (Boje 2018d).

We have explored some examples of methods of the storytelling paradigm, beginning with the self-correction induction method, and the kinds of qualitative and quantitative induction that gets us past crude induction. We looked at a Bakhtin example of narrative inquiry called stylistic dialogism, and at several quantitative induction approaches: Ethnostatistics, Qualimetrics, and critical accounting. We ended with storytelling multiplicity analyses. We reiterate there are many more methods to choose from. Here we have used a few examples to flesh out the storytelling paradigm, highlighting the role of various induction methods.

The concept of multiplicities has many intersections with the concepts of ensembles, rhizomatics, and assemblages. Later in the book we will link up a Deleuzian non-dialectical approach to Sartre's 'practical ensembles' of multiplicities (rhizomatics) with Jean Paul Sartre's (1960/2004) use of 'negation of negation' dialectic. For Deleuze and Guattari (1987), multiplicities are assemblages, and the term 'ensemble' is not used. Multiplicities are rhizomatic, with deterritorializing lines of flight.

Every story of every water-replenishment situation will be peculiar and unlike some ideal average, along innumerable aspects of the three entangled multiplicities. Coca-Cola's 'Story Map' of 248 water projects in 71 countries is not the population. Nor are we getting the 'untold stories' (Hitchin 2015) from the standpoint of the whole TamaraLand of farmers, communities of water users, policy-makers, legislators, non-human species, or the aquifers themselves. Finally, Coca-Cola justifies all this by claiming it is 'using peer-reviewed scientific and technical methods'.[2] Certainly Coca-Cola corporation is not using scientific methods of 4th Wave Grounded Theory storytelling (Boje 2019b).

Referring back to our storytelling paradigm model in Figure 4.1, we note that we have completed our discussion of the 'Method' section of this model (abstracted from Figure 4.1 and presented as Figure 4.2). We turn now to the bottom third of Figure 4.1, '*Praxes*'. We focus on research *praxes* (*theory and method in practice*) in the next chapter. Before you move to Chapter 5, you may wish to use Exercise 4.1 to practice combining qualitative and quantitative conversational storytelling interviewing (CSI).

EXERCISE 4.1   INTEGRATING QUANTITATIVE WITH QUALITATIVE IN YOUR METHODS

To integrate qualitative *with* quantitative is not the same as the classic approach to '*triangulation*' in research methods. Triangulation is defined as using more than one method to collect (inductive) data. It is a way to insure validity by using a variety of methods. There is also the triangulation of having different researchers use the same methods in different sites.

Qualimetrics, in contrast, looks at how to integrate qualitative *with* quantitative, and includes financial methods. Within the same 'conversational storytelling interview' (CSI), this can be done by asking, 'how many times' X happened, and its approximate cost. For example, if someone is absent, and the manager has to fill in to do the work, you can ask, how often it occurs, and what the manager's pay would be for those hours. If the manager is paid more than the absent worker, then that is extra cost. That is not all there is to it. If the manager is doing someone else's job, then they are not doing their own, and schedules and possibly other plans fall behind.

In the following exercise, develop CSI, and go beyond the qualitative events, to any appropriate (relatable) exploration of quantitative (frequency) and financial consequence. You can do the reverse for particular quantitative expressions (or financial claims) that emerge in the conversation. For example, if quantitative or financial data have been expressed, you might ask for related story examples or people's reactions or even predictions. If possible, give your own examples, from your own experience, as part of the back-and-forth conversational storytelling inquiry.

1.   **Write down**: What is your initiating question (preferably with your story of your related experience)?

(Example: How did your organization get into such financial difficulty that they laid off a dozen employees last month?)

2.   **Write down**: Have you had a similar experience? If not, can you think of a parallel situation, even if you have to stretch to an example where a school friend moved away, or you quit a job, or you know someone who was laid off or was a retained employee when their coworkers were laid off.

3.   If answers are all quantitative/financial, **write down** what you will ask to broaden responses to include qualitative responses.

(Example: How do the people feel who are still working here?)

4.   If answers are all qualitative, **write down** what you will ask to broaden responses to include quantitative/financial responses.

(Example: How does this compare with usual turnover rates?)

NOTE: In an actual interview, it is good to have some of these back-up questions prepared in advance but **held back** until after the person has had a chance to tell their story in their own way. The best case is that they bring up these things without prompting.

Next, Chapter 5 addresses *praxes*.

NOTES

1.   Coca-colacompany.com/stories '2017 Water Update: Investing in Water Quality and Availability' by Coca-Cola Company 24 August 2018, accessed 17 January 2019 at https://www.coca-colacompany.com/stories/2017-water.

2.   Ibid.

5. Storytelling paradigm *praxes*

In terms of research, what is '*praxis*'? After the theory and the method, '*praxis*' is how our learning (hopefully co-constructed) plays out in practical applications in the 'ground' of 'real life'. When there is a disconnect between theory, method, and *praxis*, we get an 'anomaly'. Anomalies invite us to question the validity or usefulness of the paradigm. For example, we have a belief in the precept that one ought to 'love thy neighbor'. An anomaly is something like the classic remark that the irascible Lucy delivers to famously naïve cartoon-strip-character Charlie Brown. Lucy says 'Oh, I love HUMANITY. It's just people I can't stand.' This anomaly in practice/*praxis* might cause us to reexamine our theory, our method, or our implementation for the problem apparent at the *praxis* stage.

We summarize a few storytelling paradigm anomaly-candidates in this chapter, and point out their complementarity, and end with asking, what would Peirce and Popper say? Here we focus on some examples of 'Western Ways of Knowing' (WWOK) and 'Indigenous Ways of Knowing' (IWOK) approaches to theory, method, and *praxes*. We do this because the revolution in Quantum Mechanics raises anomalies in Normal Science storytelling, many of which prompt a revival of Native Science (Cajete 2000). Native Science focused on nature's inter-connective relational ontology, and never much bought into positivism, empiricism, logical positivism, or logical empiricism, but did appreciate the IWOK-pragmatism of '*Transplanar Wisdom*' (Gladstone 2015). We do not mean to imply this is all there is to *praxis*. This discussion selects parts of *praxis* most related to our storytelling paradigm and to your research using Conversational Storytelling Interviews (CSI).

WHAT *PRAXIS*, IF ANY, ARE YOU FOCUSING UPON?

We consider the *praxis* of 'Participatory Design' (PD) inspired by the 'ontological turn' (Pihkala and Karasti 2018) as captured in relationality process ontologies (Boje 2019b), becoming posthumanist ethics (Barad 2007). There are ways of doing dissertation research in the 'ontological turn' by doing quantification *with* qualitative inquiry, for example in *praxes* such as socio-economic storytelling and critical accounts. It is not just about epistemology or positivistic empiricism, rather it is possible to tell stories with

STORYTELLING PARADIGM	WESTERN WAYS OF KNOWING **WWOK**		INDIGENOUS WAYS OF KNOWING **IWOK**	
Praxes	Socio-Economic Storytelling		Critical Accounts	Appreciative Inquiry
	Text-based Restorying	Embodied Restorying Process		
	True Storytelling			

Figure 5.1   Storytelling paradigm examples of praxes

numbers, to help numbers tell better stories, and to invoke all this to bring about changes.

PRAXIS, SARTRE, AND BRAIDED RIVERS

Considering *praxis* as a concrete experience and the application of learning, we see that it is the completion of a cycle of inquiry moving from theory to method to practice.

Make a choice:
Praxis → Theory + Method in *Practice.*
Or
Inauthentic *Praxis* → Pseudo-Theory + Pseudo-Method in Pseudo-*Practice*

What is *Inauthentic Praxis*? Knowing, Being, Doing, and Testing are inseparable, but can get reduced to Knowing dominating Being, Doing, and Testing. That means *praxis* becomes 'non-dialectical' and/or 'pseudo-dialectical' (Subject ←|→ Object Cartesian dualism) and is anything but dialogical (Sartre 1960/2004: 25). The *praxis* of historical materialism can reduce the inseparability of Knowing, Being, Doing, and Testing to just the empirical positivism such that 'dialectical Reason *creates* itself (rather than suffering itself)', and 'how can one prove that it corresponds to the dialectic of Being, without relapsing into idealism?' (ibid.). Sartre considers Marx as the *monist*, for his 'ontological monism', which consisted in affirming the irreducibility of Being to thought, and, at the same time, in reintegrating *thoughts* with the real as a particular form of human activity (ibid.). This collapse of Being into Knowing is the inductive fallacy. Collapsing Knowing into Being is the ontological fallacy (Boje 2019b). Collapsing Being and Doing into 'Knowing plus Testing' is the logical positivism fallacy. The dialectic of nature is not Marxist, but rather is the 'conception of nature just as it is, without alien addition'. Humankind is part of nature in the Baradian sociomaterialism of 'agential realism', which has the materialism of spacetimemattering without Spirit, at the Truth of Being. Sartre (1960/2004: 28) gives consideration to Testing (verification): 'Scientific laws are experimental hypotheses verified by facts; but at present, the absolute principle that "Nature is dialectical" is not open to verification at all.'

Praxis Implications of Tragedy

On 15 March 2019, in Christchurch, New Zealand, a white supremacist gunned down 50 men, women and children and wounded 50 more. A shock-wave struck the people of New Zealand and sent vibrations around the world. After the tragic event, a Muslim teenager wrote about her new understanding of leadership after seeing the heart of care of the New Zealand Prime Minister, Jacinda Ardern.[1]

> Dear Prime Minister Ardern,
> I am a 13-year-old Muslim girl from Australia and I would like to publicly share my appreciation with you. I belong to the generation that was born after 11 September 2001. I have never really contemplated how dark the anti-Muslim and anti-immigrant language is that permeates Australian society, because it is all I have ever known ...
> But then, after seeing the way you have responded to the terrorist attack in Christchurch, I realized that I now know what the role of a leader truly is. So I want to thank you on behalf of the Muslim community in this country for all that you've done since Friday. The way you have expressed support and genuine empathy for the Muslim community, and your care for the people of New Zealand as a whole, have been magnificent to see.

We attended a vigil on the University of Canterbury campus on 17 March. Thousands of faculty, students, and staff gathered. The vice-chancellor did a speech, wearing a scarf around her head, invited to do so in support of Muslim brothers and sisters. She was sending a message of support and care, asking for an end to racism, hatred, and religious intolerance. Along one side of a fence bordering the campus, cups wedged into the chain link spelled out 'Be Strong', and flowers and ribbons with messages were tied to the fence for the next few days.

World as well as local attention quickly moved from the fact of the tragedy in New Zealand to how New Zealanders reacted in its wake. Those reactions overwhelmed the story of a lone gunman, and instead highlighted the dominant values, beliefs, and norms of a caring, cohesive society. David and Grace Ann were down the road from the shooting, in a classroom building that was put on 'lockdown' by police minutes after the event. Later, a graduate student we knew who was from outside of New Zealand told us he was the closest New Zealand contact for a family of five that were killed in the mosque. He told

Grace Ann that he was impressed by how the community reacted. He said farmers offered food, everyone wanted to help. Mountains of flowers were left outside government buildings to honor the deceased. He said the event was terrible, but if it had to happen, he felt New Zealand was the best place he could have been.

Worldwide reaction to the generous and humanitarian response of the entire country of New Zealand reinforced a view of that country as an almost ideal place to live, filled with caring people in a pristine natural environment. From the concrete experience of the reaction to this tragedy (the *praxis*), people 'worked backward' to assume that, as a society, New Zealand's underlying theories and methods must be good to result in such a laudable outcome as the outpouring of sympathy and support, as well as the rectifying of laws, as a result of the tragedy in Christchurch.

David read some essays Karl Popper (2008) wrote in 1940 during his exile to New Zealand. These were the basis for Popper's (1945/2012) *The Open Society and its Enemies*. The *praxis* we witnessed and participated in were truly amazing. After 15 March 2019, those present with us at that time in New Zealand asked each other: 'Where were you during the shooting?' It was the question everyone was talking about. Clearly, as Popper (2008: 62) argues, there must be a 'spirit of cooperation, not only of Christians and non-Christians, but of [all races, ethnicities, genders], of Māoris and Pākehās, of scholars and layman, of old and young, ... a prerequisite towards building a world which is a little better than ours at present' and in 'a common effort to get nearer to the truth of what is the spirit of rationalism'.

Braided Rivers

To Angus Macfarlane (2012: 205), a spirit of cooperation 'promotes the blending of clinical and cultural streams of knowledge (affectionately named "Tō Tātou Waka" – Our Canoe) ... A blended scientific-indigenous framework (appropriately named "He Awa Whiria" – The Braided Rivers) is promoted.' We call the 'Braided River' the blending of IWOK-'Native Science' with WWOK-'Western Science' which does the zigzag of self-correcting *both/and (Big/little)* storytelling science as the 'spirit of cooperation'.

The opposite of a spirit of cooperation can appear as 'the attitude of contempt of human reason' that 'neglects criticism' (Popper 2008: 63). Our point is that there is a difference between Popper's application of a zigzag 'experimental method to [change] society' and the 'Utopian social experiment done on a large scale' in using institutions of government as a 'Utopian engineer' (Popper 2008: 58–9). Such strategies can result in a 'dangerous dogmatic attachment to a blueprint' (p. 59). Popper (ibid.) argues in a lecture in New Zealand given in 1940, that zigzag piecemeal social experiments relying on the scientific method is his preferred approach. With an attitude of humility, falli-bility, and a 'readiness to learn from mistakes' and make 'small experiments' by 'a great number of piecemeal adjustments to the various parts' of 'a great number of experiences' we are likely to have better outcomes, in Popper's view, than by following the great-leader 'megalomania tyrant' model (p. 61).

Socio-economic Storytelling and *Praxis*

Popper's is an agile, adaptive approach to small experimental practices using scientific method, and an attitude of socially responsible capitalism. This spirit of cooperation and the process of co-inquiry is also found in the 'socio-economic approach to management' (SEAM) researcher-intervenor *praxis* of Savall and colleagues (Worley et al. 2015; Savall 1975/2010; Savall et al. 2018; Savall and Zardet 2008; 2011; Savall, Zardet, and Bonnet 2008). As we discussed elsewhere, in SEAM's 'Socio-Economic Storytelling' *praxis* there are actual pre-*experiment (project)* diagnostic inquiries, hypotheses, the collection of qualitative, quantitative, and financial data interactively and in inseparability of 'Qualimetrics' rather than separately in some pseudo-mixed method or *ad hoc* triangulation.

There is a non-critical approach that has no quantification, no refutation, no falsification inquiry. In this approach, what is qualitative conforms to the principle of collecting five positive narratives for every negative one. This approach is called the 'Positive Science' of 'Appreciative Inquiry' (AI). It is what Popper (2008: 58) refers to as making sweeping organizational (or institutional) change that has unintended practical consequences: 'At present, the sociological knowledge necessary for large-scale engineering is simply non-existent.'

In short, Popper (p. 58) might wonder if AI is the positivism of 'Utopian engineering.' AI and SEAM both claim to 'fight against suffering and injus-tice' to establish some ideal dialogue between management and workers (Boje and Rosile 2003a; 2003b). Towards this end, AI seems to have almost a centralized blueprint for the ideal organization. SEAM more obviously does zigzag Diagnostic-Project-Implementation-Evaluation (DPIE) cycles of incre-mental change (Savall and Zardet 2008; Boje 2017b). They claim to unleash human potential by mastering hidden costs (akin to what critical accounting calls 'critical accounts') that give voice to the untold stories of the unheard participants.

Rather than the 'Utopian engineering' of positivism in AI, SEAM is a science applying the 'zigzag' steps of scientific method as what we in this book are calling the 'Self-Correcting Method' which includes *praxis*. SEAM applies the moral compass of socially responsible capitalism (Savall et al. 2018) to which Boje (2018a) wrote the Preface, pointing out what we term *both/and (Big/little) storytelling science.* We believe it is fair and reasonable to include SEAM's socially responsible capitalism and its 'becoming agile' (Worley et al. 2015; Boje and Cai-Hillon 2017) as a praxis of self-correction, since SEAM relies, in part, on the Triadic of induction-deduction-abduction (Boje 2016b; 2019b) of Charles Sanders Peirce. We think SEAM would not have problems with Popperian refutation, rather than just piling conjecture upon conjecture in acts of 'Crude Induction'. The traditional Positive Science movement focuses on the positive, and does not tackle the kinds of critical issues that would likely arise in critical discussion (Boje 2016d).

We join the *praxis* of 'Participatory Design' (PD) inspired by the 'onto-logical turn' (Pihkala and Karasti 2018) as captured in relationality process ontologies (Boje 2019b), becoming posthumanist ethics (Barad 2007). There are ways of doing dissertation research in the 'ontological turn' by doing quantification *with* qualitative, in *praxes* such as socio-economic storytelling and critical accounts. Next we look at Critical Accounts. As you can see in Figure 5.1, Critical Accounts falls under IWOK, because in our examples, Critical Accounts often serves the purposes of IWOK by exposing the hidden or marginalized stories behind the dominant narratives of WWOK.

CRITICAL ACCOUNTS

This refers to interventions in the public sphere done in conjunction with Critical Accounting Methods (Neu, Cooper, and Everett 2001). Critical accounts privileges voices (human and non-human) usually marginalized in traditional accounting. Critical Accounts interventions address the lack of participatory inclusion of less powerful humans and non-human *beings*. An example of including non-human beings is the climate-modelers simulation accounting work which includes the voices of nature (Boje 2016d; Stubbs, Higgins, and Milne 2013; Gray, Brennan, and Malpas 2014; Klepp and Herbeck 2016). Our point is Critical Accounts interventions (Gray, Malpas, and Brennan 2014) can give voice to voiceless communities and ecologies. An example of a critical account in the case of the Alberta intervention stressed the incomplete nature of public account data:

> We must refuse to be cowed by 'economic experts' and government 'facts', and to accept that only contracts with Albertans can be broken. By refusing to be mesmer-ized by incomplete contestable and loaded financial statements, to step beyond the figures, we can expose the 'sky is falling' ideology of deficits and debt. (Cooper and Neu 1995, p. 180, as cited in Neu, Cooper, and Everett 2001: 15)

In our own work (Smith and Boje 2011), we challenged the financial rhetoric of 'toxic assets'. The term 'toxic asset' was used to treat peoples' mortgages as 'hazardous materials', as if it was an Environmental Protection Agency (EPA) super fund cleanup of Three Mile Island. In such cases of toxic waste, there are no human wrong-doers, only tragic accidents. Similarly, the 'toxic assets' of the mortgage crisis were a tragic accident, not the fault of human wrongdoing or bankers' greed. The term 'toxic assets' served to let people hide who created these special accounting devices in the first place. Intervening to keep the public safe from dangerous toxicity puts a narrative spin on the direction of the intervention too, implying the government should be responsible for cleaning up such public problems. The term 'toxic assets' was picked up by the media, and it helped to justify the Bush administration's appeal to Congress for a $700 billion bailout of banks and mortgage security organizations. The importance here, is the toxic asset narrative was sold to the public without critical account intervention.

Both the Alberta example and the 'toxic assets' example (above) challenged prevailing accounting and financial interpretations by making visible assumptions and calculations underpinning the narrative spin. Next we turn to another type of Storytelling Praxis called Appreciative Inquiry (see Figure 5.1).

APPRECIATIVE INQUIRY

What is Appreciative Inquiry (AI)? Cooperrider and Whitney (2019: 2) answer the question:

> *Ap-pre'ci-ate, v., 1. Valuing; the act of recognizing the best in people or the world around us; affirming past and present strengths, successes, and potentials; to perceive those things that give life (health, vitality, excellence) to living systems 2. To increase in value, e.g. the economy has appreciated in value. Synonyms: VALUING, PRIZING, ESTEEMING, and HONORING.*
> *In-quire' (kwir), v., 1. The act of exploration and discovery. 2. To ask questions; to be open to seeing new potentials and possibilities. Synonyms: DISCOVERY, SEARCH, and SYSTEMATIC EXPLORATION, STUDY.*

They go on to say AI is a '**coevolutionary search for the best in people, their organizations, and the relevant world around them**' (p. 3, bold original). This is done by the key stages of Discovery, Dream, Design, and Destiny (p. 5):

> 'In AI:
> 1. **Discovery** – mobilizing a whole system inquiry into the positive change core;
> 2. **Dream** – creating a clear results-oriented vision in relation to discovered potential and in relation to questions of higher purpose, i.e. 'What is the world calling us to become?'

3. **Design** – creating possibility propositions of the ideal organization, an organization design which people feel is capable of magnifying or eclipsing the positive core and realizing the articulated new dream; and
4. **Destiny** – strengthening the affirmative capability of the whole system enabling it to build hope and momentum around a deep purpose and creating processes for learning, adjustment, and improvisation like a jazz group over time …'

All this positivity is good, but how does positivity and AI help deal with problems of colonization, white supremacy, racism, gender violence, and the destruction of the planet? AI is part of the larger 'Positive Science' movement in the Academy of Management (Cameron and Dutton 2003), and in the social sciences. AI seems to ban critical theory, deconstruction, and problem-based science from the playing field. AI collects only the *confirming* (appreciative) stories of Discovery, Dream, Design, and Destiny, by worshiping 'the power of the positive core' and 'simply … let go of accounts of the negative' for the reason that such an 'approach can lead to a negative culture' (pp. 7, 14). All is not lost. 'AI' dreams of 'Ideal Utopias' by 'Utopian social engineering' in a Utopian social engineering approach (Popper 2008: 53–4). The problem is AI's faith in 'Positive Science' becomes a theology of positive knowledge from gathering positive stories and celebrating them. This is radically different than piecemeal adaptation and change by small projects incrementally, in the zigzag self-correcting induction of SEAM (Boje 2016d).

We offer this deconstruction of the storytelling (Boje 2001) of the Positive Science movement, and its AI method.

1. What are the dualities?
2. Reinterpret the hierarchy of the duality by putting the marginalized term first.
3. Rebel Voice, tell the untold story (Hitchin 2015).
4. What is the 'Other side of the Story', the counternarratives?
5. Deny the dominant plot with counter-plots.
6. Find the exception (sometimes negative is a good thing).
7. Trace 'Between-the-lines' of 1 to 6 for essentialisms and universalisms (Boje 1995).
8. Remember to 'Resituate', by proposing a reconstruction of your deconstructions.

As Popper (2008: 47) reminds us 'The scientific devotion towards truth is itself a religious attitude' and therefore the scientific attitude of humanitarianism means doing critical dialogue and refutation, with an attitude of scientific fallibilism instead of the positive-only attitude. Otherwise, the positivism of 'Positive Science' and its method of AI means filling the bucket of knowledge with only positive stories, (or five positive stories for every negative one) in a faithful commitment to 'Positive Science' that risks becoming pseudo-science. Such positive epistemology can reduce our vision to recognize only positive ways of Being-in-the-world with repression of critical dialogue. There is a time for positivity, and a time for critical dialogue. Banning one or the other from the field of discourse has consequences (Boje, Oswick, and Ford 2004).

Figure 5.2   The bucket of knowledge

Karl Popper (1972) wrote about 'evolutionary epistemology', about how to test the statements one gathers by scientific refutation, by gathering for 'critical dialogue' before putting a conclusion into the 'Bucket of Knowledge' (Figure 5.2). Statements need to be tested, in scientific method. If we collect only positive statements in 'positive stories', then we are doing induction by repetition, dismissing refutation and critical discourse as possible ways of intervening in the deep problems of our century. Popper (1972: 7) claims: *'there is no such thing as induction by repetition'*. Putting in confirming stories, 'positive stories' is not going to result in 'True Storytelling'. It is not 'empirical reasoning'. The 'Positive Science' movement (Cameron and Dutton 2003) and the 'Positive Psychology' movement (Compton and Hoffman 2019) promises positive organizational scholarship, and AI is on that bandwagon. Flora (2019) is questioning the overly positive science movement, and proposing a bridge between the positive and the negative, while getting beyond the more superficial positivity concepts and dichotomies.

Karl Popper (1972: 12, 15–16) was an advocate of 'critical methodology', not getting polarized into pessimistic or optimistic doctrines, yet being very much against '*ad hoc* theory explanations' and *both/and (Big/little) story-telling science*. Popper applies the 'boldness of non-*adhocness*' in a '*critical method*' in a self-correcting induction of 'critical discussion' using tests that falsify a theory candidate in order to 'find a better successor'.

Perhaps AI has taken the linguistic turn too far. Karl Popper (1963: 67–8) believed theories must undergo a challenge, and disagreed with Ludwig Wittgenstein's doctrine that there are no philosophical problems, and are just

> … Pseudo-problems: that the alleged propositions or theories of philosophy are pseudo-propositions or pseudo-theories; that they are not false (if they are false, their negations would be true propositions or theories) but strictly meaningless combinations of words, no more meaningful than the incoherent babbling of a child who has not yet learned to speak properly.

In short, there are just language games. AI loads the bucket of knowledge with 'positive stories' in a language game of denial of anything that negates the institutional narrative and discourse (Boje, Oswick, and Ford 2004). This is a methodological problem and a philosophical problem. If 'positive stories' are gathered, and most negative stories ignored, then AI is a pseudo-theory, a pseudo-method, and a pseudo-*praxis*. It is pseudo-science. The AI practitioner has this principle: For every 'negative story' people in organizations tell, the AI researchers (or consultants) are instructed in their graduate education to gather five more, totally 'positive stories'. Boje (2010a: 239) observes: 'AI banishes critical theory, deconstruction, and any words of a deficit vocabulary, along with original sin' of focusing on problems, dysfunctions, in ways that upsets the managerial power hierarchy. Cooperrider (2001), for example, lists these examples as against 'positive AI science':

* Professional Vocabularies of Deficit
* Bureaucratic Disenchantment
* Original Sin
* Critical Theory
* Deconstruction
* Critical-Cynical Media.

Fortunately, there is a remedy to the positivism of 'Positive Science'. It can be coupled with 'Critical Reflexivity' and in the process, do self-correcting *both/ and (Big/little) storytelling science* (see Figure 5.3).

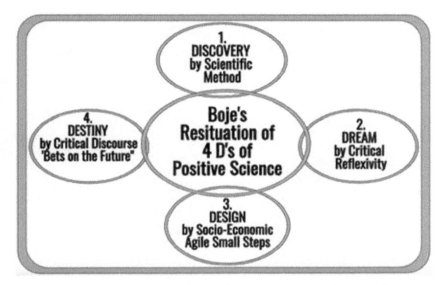

Figure 5.3   *Boje's proposed amendments to the 4Ds of Positive Science*

Karl Popper would have something to say about AI and the entire 'Positive Science' movement, in its quest for the negation of all deficit discourse. From his grave, he is pointing out the need to balance the positivism with falsification, disconfirmation, and testing of all the 'positive statements' before tossing them *ad hoc* into the 'Bucket of Knowledge'. We end up with AI Fake Storytelling, and no way to disconfirm all the pseudo-statements and pseudo-storytelling.

The good news is AI can be paired with a *both/and (Big/little) storytelling science* of critical discourse, critical conversations, critical accounts, critical reflexivity, and actual experiments in socio-economic change, and do the AI positive trip (Boje and Strevel 2016; Boje 2010a; 2011b). By doing critical theory, deconstruction, problem-based socioeconomics, and even 'Depreciative Inquiry' first, we combine disconfirming with all positivity *confirming* the four Ds, and instead of Positive Science, achieve 'Critical Real Science'.

In Depth: Why Positive Science, Appreciative Inquiry, Positive Leadership, Positive Organizational Behavior, and Positive Sociology Won't Work in Studying Racism

Jean Paul Sartre (1960/2004: 714) treats critical theory as a study of the dialectic of 'negation of the negation'. Yet Sartre's critical theory is also a story of sociomaterialism, how to study negative stories of racism, colonialism, exploitation, oppression, and the consequences of alienation and alterity, the Othering, that continues:

> Circularity – as a structure of the social as a human product – produces its intelligibility through a double determination. *On the one hand*, it is obvious that thoughts and activities are inscribed in worked matter (in so far as it produces a system of alterity through the others). This is why racism is not a mere 'psychological defense' of the colonialist, created for the needs of the cause, to justify colonization to the metropolitan power and to himself; it is in fact *Other-Thought* (*Pensee-Autre*) produced objectively by the colonial system and by super-exploitation: man is defined by the wage and by the nature of labour, and therefore it is true that wages, as they tend towards zero, and labour, as an alternation between unemployment and 'forced labour', reduce a colonized person to the sub-human which he is for the colonialist. Racist thinking is simply an activity which realizes in alterity a practical truth inscribed in worked matter and in the system which results from it.
> But, *on the other hand*, and conversely, since the elementary structures of the simplest forms *are inscribed* in inorganic matter, they refer to various activities (both past and present) which either indefinitely reproduce or have helped to produce these human *seals* as inert thoughts: and these activities are necessarily antagonistic. (Italics in original)

How can you explore the colonized person and peoples with Positive Science, when the alterity of practical truth (the evidence of the opposite) is inscribed in the worked matter (concrete evidence) of sociomateriality (Bloc 2019)? Alterity and anomaly is present in the employment practices of forced labor, such as is the case for migrant farmworkers in modern-day slavery. Enslaved workers were not being paid their true wages, and lived (and sometimes literally were chained) in squalor. They turned around their situation by organizing, forming alliances with faith groups, student groups, and doing what we call 'Ensemble Leadership' (Rosile, Boje, and Claw 2018) to develop the Fair Food program. Their approach to worker-driver corporate social responsibility creates a very 'positive story' by tackling every 'negative story' after story, and problem after problem, violence after violence, and racism after racism, in an incremental iterative approach consistent with 'negation of the negation'.

Another example of working through negative stories to create positive ones is the study of the Pākehā settlement of New Zealand and the colonization of Māori already living there. There is a need to look at the positive stories of

Māori values (Love 2017a) and the critical 'negative stories' using a critical theory standpoint (Love 2017b; 2019b; 2020). These stories consider how indigenous-Māori identities at work are shaped (Love 2018a), in not only ongoing racism, but gender in 'anteresearch' (Love 2018b). This interplay of a positive story of a peoples' survival with the negative stories of racism, sexism, and colonization culminated in Love's book (2019a), *Indigenous Organization Studies: Exploring Management Business and Community.*

In his (2018a: 2) book, Tyron Love addresses how: 'Organizations have been, and continue to be, forces of domination and suppression for indigenous peoples as well as for many other minority peoples around the world.' In short, racism goes hand in hand with indigenous people's collective struggle. Professor Love is an indigenous scholar, giving voice to 'negative stories' with stories of critical engagement of IWOK with WWOK in corporations, government, and academic systems. He examines how much Positive Science and AI can be a 'misguided product of colonization' (Love 2019a: 5). Love has important things to say about narrative/story, and how they are socially produced interpretative devices:

> Let us take the narrative/story study of indigenous managers as an example. The narratives/stories that indigenous managers produce are privileged forms of language: they are socially produced interpretive devices through which indigenous managers represent themselves, both to themselves and to others, including other workers, researchers, and so on. (Love 2019a: 21)

Love, Finsterwalder, and Tombs (2017) study Māori knowledge but not from the reductionistic, Positive Science standpoint nor from an AI into 'positive story' gathering. Our point is positive stories and AI need a context of their historical, sociological, and critical currency, by including the counternarratives, the negative stories.

Next we introduce two (2) Storytelling *Praxis* interventions based on 're-storying'. For the dissertations in a therapeutic context, there are choices between text-based restorying and embodied restorying.

Text-based Restorying

Text-based restorying is about writing out memories, telling stories about events. Text-based restorying refers to narrative therapy, White and Epston's (1990) seminal work. White and Epston limit it to only the textual practices of letters sent between family members, friends, role-models, and therapists. Social constructivists, such as Polkinghorne (2004) have sharply critiqued the notion of embodiment by arguing 'that the meaning is essentially language' and 'all human systems are linguistic systems' where 'there is nothing outside of language' (e.g., Polkinghorne 2004: 58). Polkinghorne goes so far as to argue that White and Epston's (1990) restorying processes, have no material agency, and belong only to social constructivism. Narrative displays a temporal dimension that unifies experience with a 'beginning, middle, and end' dominant governing plot that is socially supplied (Polkinghorne 2004: 58).

EMBODIED RESTORYING PROCESS

We are challenging the traditional ways of text-based restorying, so wedded to the linguistic turn. An Embodied Restorying Process (ERP) is something Grace Ann and David have been developing (Boje and Rosile 2015). We go against the social constructivist view that everything in storytelling is social language, and refer to material realms (Boje 2014: 217). Work that Grace Ann is doing (Flora et al. 2016; Rosile and Boje 2002) looks at how to do an ERP, and to effect just the kind of agency that Polkinghorne (1988; 2004) denies as possible (see Table 5.1).

Grace Ann's equine program uses work with horses that is a 100 percent on-the-ground (no riding) approach. The veteran and family first do exercises designed to help them create a communication connection with the horse. They observe the horse to discover what the horse does when they do not like something (a touch or a brushing), and what they do when they like something. Participants quickly see the connection between their bodies and the horses' bodies. When the person is nervous, the horse may often reflect nervousness. Participants quickly pick up that their own relaxation triggers a relaxed and happy attitude in the horse, so everyone is more comfortable. This helps the participants become more aware of their own bodies and emotional states. One veteran said this process felt like meditation.

After the introductory work with the horses in their stalls, participants engage in more advanced activities. They do simple tasks, such as leading the horse around an arena, and then more complex problem-solving challenges, such as leading the horse through an obstacle course of cones, barrels, and rails. Our facilitator team found that families often commented on how material objects in the horse arena (such as the halter or the stalls) or aspects of the horses themselves related to their own individual stories and family stories.

One example of embodiment happened with a veteran, wife, and daughter in a session. After seeing a horse who did not want to leave a nice indoor stall despite the open door to the outside, one veteran in the equine program commented, 'I don't think [the horse] wants to go out because out there is where all the bad things happen.' His wife and daughter laughed and said, 'just like you Dad!' and they all laughed comfortably together. Only later did Grace Ann learn about the veteran's struggle to even leave the house for daily activities as

Table 5.1   7 STEPS of embodied restorying process (ERP)

1. Recharacterize (received Organization identity) from how other organizations are telling it

2. Externalize (re-label) Make the Problem the Problem, not the Person as the problem

3. Sympathize (benefits) – of old story of or your organization has its payoffs

4. Revise (consequences) – What are the negative consequences, including the stereotypes of received organization identities being applied to you?

5. Strategize (Little Wow Moments of exception to Others' dominant master narratives); Reclaim Little Wow Moments

6. Restory (rehistoricizes the old dominant narratives by collecting Little Wow Moments into A 'New Story' of you several possibility futures), to not be stuck in the past, reliving one event

7. Publicize (support networking) e.g. letter writing, social media, celebratory events with supporters of your 'New Story' of future and potentiality, to stay in the 'new world'

he coped with flashbacks about what he referred to as 'being blown up several times' during active duty.

After the work with the horses, the families 'play' with the sand trays. Sand trays contain objects (small figures or toys) that veterans and their families assemble to depict a visual story of deployment to a combat theater. In subsequent cycles, the family may arrange the sand tray to depict a return to family life. In this way, with the small figures and objects, they embody their stories.

In sum, the ERP anchors the New Story in embodied life of the veteran's family support system. It does this by using material objects, in sand play, and in the equine-assisted growth and learning events (EAGLE), in the bigger sandplay with live horses and live people, and material objects. As Service Members and Family members tell, retell, and ultimately restory their deployment experiences, they attain more self-efficacy. They discover the self-agency to author their own story, while learning to resist and refuse the Grand Narratives such as stigma and stereotype. In each military context there are many Grand Narratives (Lyotard 1979/1984) that privilege one standpoint over any others (for example, the image and story of the Macho Warrior who refuses mental health care). And each Grand Narrative has an ideology that marginalizes others' ideologies, and discounts the living story web of relations that service members and their family members have with one another.

Next we turn to the last entry in our storytelling paradigm's *Praxes* category, True Storytelling (see Figure 5.1).

TRUE STORYTELLING

We are working with our Danish colleagues on a *praxis* called 'True Storytelling' (Boje, Larsen, and Bruun 2017; Boje 2018d). True Storytelling is about telling a story from the part of our being-ness which is connected to others. That connectedness resonates, and it is what makes the story meaningful for the listeners. This is why some stories with ethical and moral lessons are remembered and repeated, and others are not. This is what great speakers do when they establish rapport with their audience: they elicit the feeling of recognition, of coming home, in the listeners. It is easy to communicate the principles of True Storytelling. It is about being ethically true, as opposed to the fake-news, fake leaders, fake presidents, and their fake storytelling. We offer seven (7) principles of True Storytelling (ibid.).

Seven True Storytelling Principles

1. Truth: **You yourself must be true and prepare the energy and effort for a sustainable future.**
2. Make room: **True storytelling makes spaces respecting the stories already there.**
3. Plot: **You must create stories with a clear plot creating direction and help people prioritize.**
4. Timing: **You must have timing.**
5. Help stories along: **You must be able to help stories on their way and be open to experiment.**
6. Staging: **You must consider staging, including scenography and artifacts.**
7. Reflection: **You must reflect on the stories and how they create value.**

'True Storytelling' is possible if and only if every 'Fake Storytelling' premise and false conclusion is challenged as an incomplete story, so we search the other side of the untold story (Hitchin 2015). By this self-correcting process, by the trial and error of the scientific method, we arrive closer to the truth (Popper 1963: 318). As with Peircean self-correcting induction, it is all about doing testing, since we researchers suffer from fallibilism, and learning from mistakes is how we get closer to True Storytelling (Boje 2018d). In sum, this comes close to a self-correcting induction, which Peirce saw as a potential methodology to resolve the problem of inductive fallacy (Boje 2019b).

In Depth: Schopenhauer

When we try to determine 'True Storytelling' by refuting 'Fake Storytelling', sometimes this reveals nihilism, whereby 'it now seems there is no meaning at all in existence, as if everything were in vain', except for the 'will to live' (Hitchin 2015). We may try to escape the nihilism, with Schopenhauer, by going into the fine arts. However, there is a method of self-correcting we can use to get closer to True Storytelling. Schopenhauer gives up on the fake storytelling of, shall we say, business logic, and mechanistic science, and follows two different pathways. One, mentioned above, is an escape into artistic fine arts (which is quite ironic given what is happening to higher education in the purge of humanities). The second pathway is following the Maya, who are aware of the 'veil of deception', and those in India offering the ancient wisdom of the Vedas and Puranas (Sanskrit: पुराण purāṇa). Neither pursuit of form without ground, or ground without form can explain the *qualitates occultae*, that which remains unfathomable after we observe the manifest *spacetimemattering* of things. These *occult qualities* and *enchantments* are not accessible to human intellect. Both the arts and the spiritual mystics offer pathways to escape the 'Fake Storytelling' Schopenhauer finds in the sciences and the practical (politics, business, etc.). Schopenhauer finds these realms filled with the struggle of wills, a striving. This project is to go beyond the dualism of subject and object of Descartes, as well as to go beyond Kant's placement of space and time into the *a priori*. Then we have the surprise: his alternative is 'the condition of multiplicity' (Schopenhauer 1928: 5). His book is about

STORYTELLING PARADIGM	WESTERN WAYS OF KNOWING **WWOK**			INDIGENOUS WAYS OF KNOWING **IWOK**	
THEORY	Quantum Storytelling Theory				
	Narrative Retrospective Sensemaking	Narrative-Counternarrative Dialectics		Living Story Dialogisms	
				Ensemble Leadership Theory	
	Antenarrative Prospective Sensemaking				
	2nd Wave Grounded Theory	3rd Wave Grounded Theory		4th Wave Grounded Theory	1st Wave Grounded Theory
METHOD	Self-Correcting Induction Method				
	Quantitative Induction	Qualitative Induction			Crude Induction
	Narrative Quantification	Ethno-statistics	Qualimetrics	Critical Accounting	
PRAXES	Storytelling Multiplicities Analyses				
	Socio-Economic Storytelling			Critical Accounts	Appreciative Inquiry
	Text-based Restorying	Embodied Restorying Process			
	True Storytelling				

Figure 5.4   *The entire storytelling paradigm examples in 'Braided River' co-grounding cross paradigm authentication*

multiplicities, and how we constitute the world as idea, yet we can sense we have bodily existence in relation to Heraclitus' 'eternal flux of things' (p. 9).

Now we can put the storytelling paradigm explorations together.

Angus Macfarlane (2012: 206) has suggested a way to blend IWOK and WWOK *both/and (Big/little) storytelling science* (see Figure 5.4). This blending uses the Māori scholar's Kaupapa Māori method of New Zealand, and the Pākehā (descendants of European settlers') conventional program evaluation and development methods. Macfarlane asserts both can work together to 'co-*ground*' knowledge using 'The Braided Rivers' (*He Awa Whiria*) approach and doing *shared authentication*:

> … shared authentication may be generalized into settings and situations where educational and psychological practice works in the best interests of Māori – the indigenous people of Aotearoa New Zealand, and Pākehā – descendants of European settlers.

What we add to 'The Braided River' approach is to use refutation testing as part of the shared authentication approach.

In the spirit of *praxis*, we offer an exercise on action steps to continue your research and promote your career as a scholar.

EXERCISE 5.1   *PRAXIS* – CONTINUING YOUR RESEARCH AFTER YOUR ORAL DEFENSE

After or just before your oral defense, you can begin preparing the following ways to extend your work.

Do one or all of the things listed below.

REHEARSE

Write out, time your delivery, and **practice** the following:

1. A **one-sentence** summary (not an overly long sentence!) of the main point of your research.
2. A **one-minute** summary of your research.
3. An **under-3-minutes** summary of your research (the length of a film trailer).
4. Make a **VIDEO** of one of the above. Get films students to help or hire a professional film editor.

RELEASE

Post the written descriptions and/or your video on-line, with or without a full resume. Consult those who know how to post but restrict access, if you like, to only those who have permission. Consider Linked-In, and other sites related to your field.

RESEARCH and write down OUTLETS for your dissertation research, based on:

1. Implications of your findings;
2. Extensions possible with your research;
3. Ease/speed of publication (can be used as a base to cite in articles targeted to more elite outlets);
4. Top-rated journals in the field of your research (it does not hurt to aim high, but do not restrict yourself to those journals);
5. Search ESPECIALLY for 'Special Issue' volumes that are or could be linked to your research;
6. Conference proceedings and even just presentations (these can be referenced in other papers).

PRACTICE YOUR DELIVERY

1. To your peers,
2. At your home institution,
3. At conferences,
4. At job interview.

PROMOTE YOURSELF

1. Write a press release about you and your research. Find a Journalism or English Writing grad student and pay them to help you. Include interesting personal angles to make your story appealing, human, interesting, fun!
2. Get feedback on your press release from faculty or classmates before releasing it.

PARTICIPATE

1. Identify sub-groups, local conferences, and on-line groups interested in your topic.
2. Search bibliographies and footnotes in published articles related to your topic, and contact key people whose work you admire. Contact them (email or write first and follow up with a phone call) and tell them

how much you admire their work (be specific, show you have read and understood it), ask for pointers on how to proceed or ask them to recommend others working in your area, or what they think are future directions, almost anything to establish a connection.

3. Volunteer to help at your local and national professional organizations – they always need help!

4. Look beyond your discipline to related ones, for example, Business Administration has overlapping areas with Public Admin, Educational Admin, and Hotel, Restaurant, and Tourism.

5. Check out the versions of your professional group in other countries, for example, Business Administration folks go to the Academy of Management, the British Academy of Management (BAM), Irish Academy of Management, European Group for Organization Studies, the Standing Conference on Organizational Symbolism (SCOS), the International Association of Cross-Cultural Communication and Management (IACCM), the Institute for SocioEconomic Research (ISEOR) in France. Contact the association leaders for advice on who is working in your area.

6. Contact your own University's present and past faculty and alumni.

PLAN WITH ACTION AND ACCOUNTABILITY

1. Write down your next step with a completion date. You can have more than one next step, but NOT more than three. Add steps as you complete items.

2. Get someone to witness and sign your action plan, preferably someone who will be interested in hearing updates at least weekly.

NOTE

1. Newsroom.com 'An Open Letter to Jacinda Ardern', Johan, Summer, 21 March 2019, accessed 22 March 2019 at https://www.newsroom.co.nz/2019/03/21/499320/an-open-letter-to-jacinda-ardern?fbclid=IwAR1C85fu4bPl3jI21dwGC1bpCPEfdf-FxYZGiTYQxrEmvzXQ45bbCE6kO6w.

6. Why Karl Popper is rolling over in his grave

KARL POPPER'S STORY

Karl Popper, born in Vienna 1902 received his PhD from the University of Vienna. Malachi Hacohen (2000) gives an historical account of Karl Popper's formative years, and includes Popper's attempt to kill off the 'logical positivism' (and logical empiricism) movement of the 1920s, developed by members of the Vienna Circle, including Rudolf Carnap and Moritz Schlick, among others. This was Popper's lifelong struggle, which was ironic, because Popper could not find support for his own theories of induction outside the Vienna Circle. They never accepted his standpoint, but were the only ones helping him to publish instead of perish completely. It is ironic, as well, because instead of subscribing to logical positivism, Popper remained throughout his career a *'metaphysical realist'* in this *theory-method-praxis,* which we will explain in this chapter.

Popper was exiled for nine years (1938–1945) to New Zealand, to Canterbury College of the University of New Zealand, where he worked to get his only book *Logik der Forschung* (1935) translated to English. This did not happen until 1959 (*The Logic of Scientific Discovery*), over a decade after his time in New Zealand. While in New Zealand, Popper (1945/2012) wrote his book *The Open Society and its Enemies*, to deal with Nazism, The Third Reich, the holocaust, and the anti-Semitism of Austria. The book was also about how he was definitely not a logical positivist. He continued revising the book, and then wrote a post-scripting (1945/2008) *After the Open Society: Selected Social and Political Writings.*

Finally, in this chapter, we will follow up on how Popper's (1978) 'Three Worlds' lecture can be retheorized, but not exactly refuted by Penrose (2011), the quantum physicist, staying between the Three Worlds. Popper's (1956/1982) postscript to his earlier German work, *Logik der Forschung* (*The Logic of Scientific Discovery*) is his deconstruction of about every quantum theory and every quantum method, and every quantum *praxis* that has been attempted until 1982. We will reserve this discussion until Chapter 7 of this book.

How did we become so familiar with, and such big fans of, Karl Popper? We (Grace Ann and David) were in New Zealand as Visiting Erskine Fellows at the University of Canterbury for the entire month of March 2019. In the house where we stayed on the campus, someone left a discarded book, left along with novels and travel guides to New Zealand. The book was written by Karl R. Popper (1963). It was titled *Conjectures and Refutations: The Growth of Scientific Knowledge*. David devoured the book, and got Sabrina Dadder, doctoral student, to check out all eight volumes of Charles Peirce (1933–1937) so he could see how Popper was approaching the problem of self-correction.

At the Erskine Fellows reception, we met the graduate dean, Bryce Williamson, who knew several emeritus professors who had taught Popper. David arranged to meet one of them, Andy Pratt, on 8 March. That day David chased down some books, not in the main library, but strangely placed in the Engineering Library. Mark van der Klei, another doctoral student, was kind enough to check them out. One of these was Popper's (1994) *The Myth of the Framework,* which we highlight in Chapter 3. But there was another rare find: it was a set of lecture notes on Popper's (1945) talk to the University of Otago.[1] The notes were typed on a typewriter. When Bryce brought Andy to the Faculty Club for an introduction, Andy asked David, 'Did you check out the book?'

> David: 'Which book is that?'
> Andy: 'The lecture notes from Popper, 1945.'
> David: 'Yes, I have it. It's amazing.'
> Andy: 'There is a story to tell of Popper and Sir John Carew Eccles.'

SIR JOHN CAREW ECCLES' STORY

The Faculty Club was noisy with beer and tea drinkers as we listened to this story. Popper was giving a presentation one day in 1945. In the audience was Eccles, before he became a Nobel prizewinner. Popper spotted Eccles in the audience that day. Eccles was a chemist who had a theory of electrical forces, but he had a problem: a theory of chemical forces was overtaking his theoretical framework. Popper's advice was for Eccles to do a refutation of his theory of electrical bonds.

Eccles took the advice seriously, and developed instrumentation to do experiments to refute his own theory. And it was this work Eccles did in New Zealand, refuting his own theories, for which he earned a Nobel Prize in 1963, for work as a neurophysiologist. While others, such as Rutherford, earned Nobel Prizes, Eccles was the only one who did it in New Zealand at the University of Otago (1952–1962)! Eccles was by birth Australian, but he did the science of refutation in New Zealand with colleagues there. In the book

Facing Reality, Eccles (1970/2013: 105) says he fully accepts the philosophical achievements of Sir Karl Popper:

> At that time I learned from Popper that it was not scientifically disgraceful to have one's hypothesis falsified. That was the best news I had had for a long time. I was persuaded by Popper, in fact, to formulate my electrical hypotheses of excitatory and inhibitory synaptic transmission so precisely and rigorously that they invited falsification – and, in fact that is what happened to them a few years later, very largely by my colleagues and myself, when in 1951 we started to do intracellular recording from motor neurons. Thanks to my tutelage by Popper, I was able to accept joyfully this death of the brain-child which I had nurtured for nearly two decades and was immediately able to contribute as much as I could to the chemical transmission story which was the Dale and Leowi brain-child.

It was Popper he thanks for getting him out of the dualism of Cartesianism and into the triadic interactionism of Three Worlds. 'World 1' is Physical Objects, 'World 2' is States of Consciousness, but beyond the body-mind split is 'World 3', Knowledge in the objective sense as a way to solve scientific problems using critical arguments.

Here are some excerpts from Sir John Carew Eccles (1945, underlining in original). These are taken from his lecture notes on Popper's Principles of Scientific Method, which was a series of five lectures:

All science has this character, which may be summarized as follows
  LECTURE I: The Hypothetical Deductive Method: (p. 1)
(1) All scientific statements retain this hypothetical character (hypotheticism). They are always hypotheses. Certainty is not, and cannot be the aim of science.
(2) Deductivism – the so-called inductive method is a kind of optical illusion. It looks like induction, but never is.
(3) Testing of theories. Doctrine concerning the way we test our theories (see Lecture II).
  LECTURE II: Testing of Theories: (p. 3)
  Essence of Scientific Method: One puts up a hypothesis, a guess, a leap into the unknown, and from this one deduces consequences and then tests these ... We can call this view falsificationism, i.e. one adopts a hostile attitude to the hypothesis...
  For example, the famous Aristotelian deduction – 'All men are mortal, Socrates is a man, therefore Socrates is mortal' (p. 3) ...
  But if the theory is that all men are immortal, then the first dead man refutes the theory. That is, we can falsify a theory, but never prove it: (p. 4) ...
  You don't need to throw the theory away. (p. 4) ...
  However, the people who produce a theory generally take the attitude that they wish to verify a theory. That is an easy attitude. A testing is left to others (p. 5) ...
  An important point is the question of the ad hoc hypothesis which is introduced to avoid falsification of a theory ... However, if one makes an addition to an ad hoc

hypothesis that can be tested by other means, then it becomes an hypothesis ... The better conclusion is that the first ad hoc hypothesis is falsified (p. 5)...

An 'ad hoc' hypothesis has no other action but to explain the series of facts it was invented for. <u>A proper hypothesis has other consequences which can be tested in order to attempt to falsify it.</u> This is the new and different attack on the method of induction, for induction would only lead to ad hoc hypotheses, and these lead no where, i.e. process of induction is of no interest scientifically (p. 5)...

The real method of science is the reverse – it is to risk hypotheses, which are not lies, as their hypothetical nature is recognized (p. 6) ...

Eccles (1945: 7–8) includes these four diagrams, which we have reconfigured into one (Figure 6.1). Eccles listened to Popper about refuting his own theory of synapse, and developed a test to do so, and that won him the 1963 Nobel Prize in Physiology or Medicine.

Next we want to show how a self-correcting process (inspired by Eccles' ideas drawn from Popper's lectures) relates to auxiliary assumptions.

AUXILIARY ASSUMPTIONS AND DAVID TRAFIMOW'S STORY

David Trafimow (2003; 2012; 2018; 2019) shows the importance of auxiliary assumptions in theory testing. We do not test all auxiliary assumptions at once. We select some to test in each phase, learn from that, and select new ones to investigate. It is important to try to falsify (and refute) the theories we deduce, and the abductive-hypotheses we put forth. Otherwise, we are only doing verification without refutation, and that is the major inductive fallacy that plagued the first three waves of Grounded Theory. 'A prediction is not derived solely on the basis of a theory but rather from the combination of a theory and assumptions that are not part of the theory' (Trafimow 2017: 216).

> These assumptions are often termed auxiliary hypotheses or auxiliary assumptions. I will use auxiliary assumptions so as to include what some philosophers considered to be 'initial conditions' ... as well as assumptions that link nonobservational terms in theories with observational terms in empirical hypotheses (e.g., Trafimow and Uhalt 2015). (Trafimow 2017: 216)

In Figure 6.1 we are combining Trafimow's (2012; 2017) work on auxiliary assumptions with the Peirce's (1931/1960) writing on self-correcting using the Abductive-Inductive-Deductive (AID) triadic. The area outside the set of embedded triangles represents successive self-correcting AID phases of the research project. The figure depicts the sets of auxiliary assumptions which are accounted for in particular inductive tests, abductive-hypotheses, and deductive theories (represented in the successive triangles). There are assumptions you have not yet included or investigated (designated as such in the figure) in

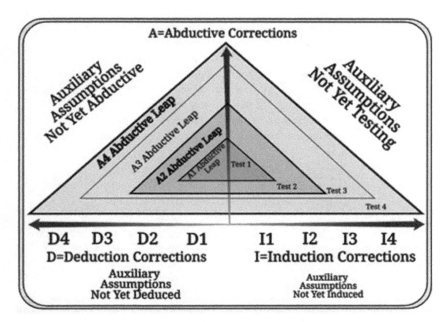

Figure 6.1   Self-correcting and auxiliary assumptions

successive self-correcting phases of a research project. We look at four kinds of assumptions, one by one, with the caveat that they are entangled, inter-dependent, and not independent from one another.

1. **Abductive Assumptions:** First, there are some auxiliary assumptions stemming from your abductive-hypotheses.
2. **Inductive Assumptions:** Second, there are some auxiliary assumptions related to Peirce's four tests of induction. Recall that the four inductive tests are
   1. Challenging some of your own theory by self-reflexivity, for example using thought experiments;
   2. Do Conversational Storytelling Interviews thereby bringing in other people to test your assumptions;
   3. Research other sciences than your own to see if other tests that have been reported are available; and
   4. If the first three tests are not sufficient, do an actual experiment or an actual intervention (a field experiment such as used with SEAM, or 'refutation interviews' to challenge your own assumptions as per-formed by van der Klei, described in Chapter 4).

3. **Deductive Assumptions:** Third, recall that your theories are your deductions from literature or from your own cognitive reasoning skills. Keep in mind there are some auxiliary assumptions that are related to your theories. There are some nonobservational terms (like values, attitudes, or beliefs), for which we create assumption sets. 'Terms' are words in your hypothesis that represent another theory, and that theory can carry with it some additional assumptions, which are more of our 'auxiliary assumptions'.

4. **Unexamined Assumptions:** Finally there are the unexamined auxiliary assumptions you have not attended to in a round of self-correcting AID.

EXERCISE 6.1 AUXILIARY ASSUMPTIONS AND SELF-CORRECTING CONVERSATIONAL STORYTELLING INTERVIEWS

Using Abduction, choose a topic of research of interest to you. If you already have a research topic, you may use it. If not, for practice, you may reproduce the research sequence described below using the topic of the weather, or you may choose your own practice topic.

We offer a simple hypothetical example relating to the weather. We start with Abduction. I am curious to know what the weather will be like tomorrow. I have an idea that at least I can predict that it will not snow in July. I base this induction on my personal experience. It has never snowed in July in all my many years of life. I decide to interview some people about their experience of the weather in July. I call my mother.

My mother says she has never known it to snow in July. This is an inductive test using conversational storytelling. Before ending our phone call, my mother tells me about a day in the 1950s when the sky went completely dark in the middle of the afternoon, and she never found out why. Later I google this and find on-line reports of this 'mystery'. I decide this subject will need to wait for a different research project.

(Consider: what is 'relevant' to my topic, what is irrelevant, and what are potentially important diversions or anomalies?)

Next I begin a process of asking every student who stops into my office on campus about the weather. We are in New Mexico, so I begin with casual comments, like 'Is it hot enough for you?' We exchange comments about the weather, eventually getting to their experience of the weather in July.

(Consider: what sort of sample is this? Are there any potential dangers or pitfalls of this sample?)

One of my interviewees is a student from Nepal. He tells me that at home, you can always see snow in the mountain peaks. Now I can identify an auxiliary assumption: I have assumed a location that is not too high in altitude. This thought leads me to consider other aspects of the physical location. I decide to also specify that the location needs to be in the northern hemisphere.

(Consider: have I overlooked aspects of place, of physical location? Of the natural environment?)

I adjust my original theory based on my inductive tests (the interviews). Now my theory is that it never snows in July at sea level in the temperate zones of the northern hemisphere. This is also an interesting example of how Western Ways of Knowing (WWOK) can tend to ignore the importance of physical place, which is much more important in Indigenous Ways of Knowing (IWOK).

Next I talk with a student who tells me about the time in New Mexico that it hailed in July. Now I wonder: Does hail count as snow? My choice on this will constitute an example of deductive corrections to a theory.

(Consider: what is the impact of my choice and definition of 'terms'? Am I allowing the 'linguistic turn' to overshadow the 'ontological turn'?)

Finally: What do I tend to overlook, and what questions do I want to be sure to ask, in my current or next research project?

In Popper's version of what Peirce calls the self-correcting induction method, the process involves refutation of 1st hypothesis, and then successive leaps in *ad hoc* hypotheses by providing for testability. This is the Popperian way to move beyond 1st, 2nd, and 3rd Wave Grounded Theory to 4th Wave of *both/ and (Big/little) storytelling science*. As with Peircean self-correcting induction, it is all about doing testing, since we researchers suffer from fallibilism, and learning from mistakes is how we get closer to True Storytelling.

THE 'LOGICAL POSITIVIST LEGEND' ABOUT KARL POPPER

A Vienna Circle narrative about Karl Popper being a 'logical positivist' became known far and wide as the 'Positivist Legend' (Hacohen 2000: 208–10). The legend was possible to spread that Popper was a positivist because Popper often 'withdrew into seclusion for lengthy periods, then reappeared to confront the circle with new ideas' and the circle gave him 'critical feedback' to develop the ideas (Hacohen 2000: 209). Most historians just have accepted the Vienna Circle's side of the story without investigating the counterstories.

The Vienna Circle's 'Grand Narrative' said: 'Popper exaggerated his disagreements with positivism' (p. 209). Positivism is defined here, in this book, as doing confirmations and accumulating sightings of agreement, while not attempting to disconfirm one's own theory-method-*praxis*. Popper's untold story, and the counternarrative to 'Grand Narrative' of the Vienna Circle, is that he had refused to take the linguistic turn that the Vienna Circle championed, and instead constructed a problem focus. Popper was a post-Kantian (neo-Kantian) trying to prevent the Vienna Circles' *linguistic turn* to Wittgenstein from contaminating metaphysics. Popper also kept shooting himself in the foot because his personality had several tragic flaws: 'He was brilliant, but self-focused, both insecure and arrogant, irascible and self-righteous. He was a terrible listener, and bent on winning arguments at all costs' (Hacohen 2000: 209). His nemesis, the Vienna Circle, was congenial, hospitable, and people liked them.

It seems Popper lacked the political skill to change the Philosophy of Science paradigm of logical positivism and its Logical Empiricism of the Vienna Circle members. Such was the group dynamics that while Popper kept his focus on paradigm differences, the Vienna Circle kept insisting there was mainly common ground. His seminal work (Popper 1935) *Logik der Forschung* was not translated from the original German until 1956. At that time, it was translated to English as *The Logic of Scientific Discovery*.

During the early years with the Circle, Popper's work in German was appropriated by the logical positivists in order to further their own movement. At the same time, the Circle was rejecting (or downplaying) the foundation-shaking aspects of Popper's framework. 'Popper they claimed belonged to their movement' (Hacohen 2000: 211). Popper's counternarrative was that the Vienna Circle had plagiarized his philosophy while obscuring its revolutionary implications, and thus the 'legend of a positivist Popper would emerge' in the storytelling while the counternarrative would not see the light of day (Hacohen 2000: 211).

Popper (1956/1983: 140) says 'for neither a deductive nor an inductive inference can ever proceed from consistent premises to a conclusion that formally contradicts their premises'. Popper (1956/1983: 149) claims he is a '*metaphysical realist*' doing 'metaphysical realism' (p. xxv), and engages in the humility of fallibilism by doing testability, refutability, and falsifiability of inferences (p. 175). Finally he strongly objected to the Vienna Circle's logical positivism (Popper 1956/1983: 175). Note that the last part of this chapter discusses Popper and Peirce and their views on why we researchers are metaphysicians. The section is sub-titled 'We are all metaphysicians'.

Both Karl Popper and Charles Sanders Peirce are refuting theory-method-*praxis* by deconstructing the metaphysics denied by 'Big S Big Science' and preferring the fallibilism humility of 'little s little science'. Peirce and Popper are not just being disagreeable.

Rather, what was important to Popper was the '*critical discussion*' in science, so that the 'heart of the reason of sense' (Popper 1956/1983: 175–6) could demarcate empirical science on the one hand and, on the other hand, pseudo-science, metaphysics, logic, and pure mathematics. But he stressed that meaningful theories are on both sides of the demarcation. In short, metaphysics can be meaningful, and much of the science-knowledge development, such as atomism eventually becoming quantum physics, began with Democritus' metaphysics inferences long before tests of refutation or falsification could be enacted in the Copenhagen Interpretation. Popper concludes:

> I can only say that I have always severely criticized positivism and I have never changed my mind in this matter ... I am resigned to the fact that, in spite of this, this label will stick to me to the end of my days. (Popper 1956/1983: 177)

This brings us to his time in New Zealand.

Karl Popper, to avoid both the Vienna Circle and the German invasion of Austria, exiled himself to Christchurch, New Zealand in 1937, and stayed in exile until 1945, after World War II. During Popper's nine years of exile, his work that was in German (1935) did not get translated by an English publisher until 1959, *The Logic of Scientific Discovery*, after his New Zealand time (as we mentioned above). He was very concerned about this lack of a translation. Meanwhile, Popper stressed the need for scientific research in his teaching. His teaching post was within the Canterbury College at the University of New Zealand, which later became the University of Canterbury.

During his time at Canterbury College, Popper sent a letter to the New Zealand government advising them to be begin funding faculty and student research if New Zealand was actually serious about developing scientists (Allen et al. 1945).[2] The two-page document became known as 'the Canterbury Declaration' and was a watershed moment in doctoral student education (Clark 2005). Clark (2005) says Popper's legacy, and the Canterbury Declaration, research must inform teaching educators for a number of very good reasons:

> First, students are entitled to be informed of the very latest or the very best ideas and findings about past and present educational theories, policies and practices... (Clark 2005: 116)

> Second, on most educational topics of interest to teacher educators and their students, there is widespread national disagreement about how to conceptualize any particular problem or issue, how to theorize about it, what evidence is relevant to

it, how the evidence is to be collected and assessed, which policies best state the desired ends, and what practices are best suited to achieve such goals. (p. 117)

Thirdly, intellectual liberty demands, from academic staff in particular, but no less from their students, a confrontation with the dash of ideas, of entering into rational dialogue and critical analysis where all ideas, favored or not, are subject to the harshest and most rigorous criticism and, if found wanting, refuted. (p. 118)

Fourthly, as teacher educators, our teaching is to be research-based and if we are to be in an informed position to assist our students to read, assess and critique, even reject, the research they read, then we ourselves must be knowledgeable about not only the content of the research, the substantive arguments and findings about this or that, but also about the adequacy of the research and its methodology. (p. 119)

ARE POPPER AND ECCLES ROLLING OVER IN THEIR GRAVES?

We are wondering if Sir Popper and Sir Eccles are, reading these four points from the Canterbury Declaration, now both rolling over in their graves. We can hear the bones rattling, the earth is moving … To be fair, Clark (2005) does criticize the performativity of the new ways of assessment, but limits his critique to teacher education, missing the substance of Popper's, Eccles' and colleagues' critique of the importance of actually funding doctoral education in all sciences.

> … the ranking of the six universities with major programs in Education are problematic. The first four (excluding Lincoln) are all single units separate from their local colleges of education, whereas Waikato and Massey are multi-department merged units … (Clark 2005: 122)

Peter Roberts (2013) includes Clark's reference to the 'Canterbury Declaration', which Clark reduces to a focus on preparing teachers in teacher education. The problem we want to raise is that there is a bigger and deeper problem that Roberts calls 'academic dystopia', how performativity (á la Lyotard) has crept into New Zealand's category of 'tertiary education'. In particular, instead of the 'Canterbury Declaration' as the basis for our science funding, there is the Performance-Based Research Fund (PBRF). It is an example of Lyotard's worst performativity nightmare.

The term '*tertiary education*' is employed in New Zealand to cover all post-secondary education institutions, from universities and polytechnics through private training establishments. With PBRF comes academic dystopia, and the worst fears of computerized digital education in the postmodern world (Boje and Dennehy 1993). It is the commodification of knowledge, and its knowledge workers are we the academics (Boje 2018c). We are ruled by multinational corporations that influence the education process. This commercialization of knowledge fits a grand narrative of progress by a tech-noscientific efficiency (heavy emphasis on *efficiency*). The technical apparatus requires investment, and we academics are the surplus value, which needs evermore-increased performance outcomes (Boje 2018c). Instead of research funds for our science, science is reduced to a performative force of production and consumption, to effect wealth by efficiency.

> It was more the desire for wealth than the desire for knowledge that initially forced upon technology the imperative of performance improvement and product realization. The 'organic' connection between technology and profit preceded its union with science. Technology became important to contemporary knowledge only through the mediation of a generalized spirit of performativity. Even today, progress in knowledge is not totally subordinated to technological investment. (Lyotard 1979/1984: 45, as cited in Roberts 2013)

Knowledge is served á la carte by knowledge professors in the commodity system, in the new virtual universities where everything, the libraries, the student training, the student responses, the professor ratings, the outcomes assessments, are all digitized. PBRF ends up being the ultimate grand narrative of legitimation, and what Popper (1994) calls 'The Myth of the Framework' which has no counternarratives, no counter examples, only confirmation without disconfirmation with scientific methodology.

The global knowledge society has turned into a knowledge economy, deploying more and more deeply problematic systems of performative meas-urement (Roberts 2013). We are being quantified into citation counts, evaluation scores, and now into reputation scores. This is a neoliberal social reconstructivism that has the authors of the Canterbury Declaration rolling over in their graves. Instead of our science funding there is utility maximizing in knowledge commodification.

Popper was a critic of 'The Myth of the Framework' and an ethical con-science of society.

Meantime, while Popper was working to promote refutations and research funding of pure science projects, as part of New Zealand higher education, the 'logical positivist narrative' became a widespread legend, a veritable mythology that persisted and plagued Popper for the rest of his days until he retired in 1969 from the London School of Economics, and even after his death in 1994. With the English publication of *The Logic of Scientific Discovery*, Popper hoped the mythology would vanish. His main critique of logical posi-tivism, however, was not published until 1979, *Die beiden Grundprobleme der Erkenntnistheorie*. It was published in German and did not appear in English for a very long time. Finally, in 2014, *The Two Fundamental Problems of the Theory of Knowledge* was published in English. Popper (1979/2014: 47) asks: '*Critique of strict positivism – twofold transcendence of natural laws. Can* empirical statements be universally valid ... solely on the basis of experience?' His answer: No. Strict positivism (not to be confused with logical positivism) 'abandons the strict universality of natural laws' and therefore cannot preserve the 'strictly universal thesis' and instead its empirical statements ... can be valid only on the basis of experience' (p. 47).

From the above quote we see the contradiction of a strict empiricist claiming the universality of natural laws, but appending them in favor of sensory experience, and conceding to the classical rationalism of 'the *a priori* validity of the principle of induction' (p. 47). In short, immanence of experience and transcendent universal are in contradiction, but without the Kantian transcendental critique methodology (p. 63). In self-correcting induction, the Peircean method of testable conjectures privileges refutation as the basis of scientific inquiry.

Popper is hard hitting against the Vienna Circle's linguistic turn (p. 85): 'The most eminent proponents of logical positivism such as Carnap, Schlick and Wittgenstein ... base their epistemological investigations on a concept of knowledge completely different from Kant's.' In other words, for Popper, logical positivism has erred in how it poses the problem of induction, by a quantum leap into deductive universal laws. This happens without an actual test of natural laws, and is accompanied by a retreat into empirical statements (abstract-schemata of boxes imprisoning concepts with arrows between them). The result is the pure conceptual domain of logical positivism, particularly in 2nd Wave Grounded Theory and 3rd Wave Grounded Theory ontological relativism of social constructivism (see Chapter 8) that does not solve the underlying epistemology of knowledge questions (Boje 2019b). Nor does 1st Wave Grounded Theory, its 'Crude Induction', resolve these issues by invoking pure intuition (abduction).

Peircean abduction does not test Popperian refutations of the conjectures, nor engage in Peircean self-correcting induction tests. Abduction does not consider how induction snowball samples differ from the entire population, but generalizes anyway, in some morphologic typology, or in an etiology of correlatives or causes by excessive empirical coding routines of interview interrogations. This is typically combined with first inductive tests by acts of self-reflexivity upon the researcher's own experience of their classifications *post hoc*. The result is what Popper (1979/2014: 214) calls '*pseudo-statement* positions' in the logical positivism '*concept of meaning*' in a science that is '*nonsensical*' but absolutely 'grammatically correct' in Wittgenstein and in the Vienna Circle's linguistic turn.

Popper's (1979/2014: 304) main critique is the '*problem of induction:* What is the relationship between the logical positivist concept of meaning, and the distinction between strictly universal and singular statements?' Answer: a reductionism from universal and singular statement classification to an experiential condition, and then by several quantum leaps to universal states of affairs justified as any Schopenhauerian would attest on typology-classification (morphology) regularities, or by an etiological grand narrative, without counternarrative challenges. In *both/and (Big/little) storytelling science* every statement or gesture of storytelling is indexical to a state of affairs in *spacetimemattering* and the clash of paradigms.

For Popper's (1956/1983) critique of logical positivism, he 'declares natural laws to be pseudo-statements'. In the same book, in his 1956 Preface, he says: 'Scientific method does not exist' and he asserts that the 'myth of the subject' is as ephemeral as the search for 'true theory' and 'scientific truth' (p. 5). He adds: 'there is no method of ascertaining the truth of a scientific hypothesis, i.e., no method of verification' (p. 6). He recommends an 'abandonment of the quest for rational explanation' (p. 57). This is why Popper had attacked 'Science with a capital "S"' (p. 13).

Popper is a 'critical metaphysician' declaring method is metaphysical, and declares he is doing what he calls 'metaphysical realism' (p. 80) especially after his review of 'quantum theory' (p. 126). We hope you can see how logical positivism (positivism, and post-positivism apologetics) privileges WWOK-science over IWOK's Native Science, in which forces of nature are active, and people, animals, fish, water, and rocks are part of nature in a place, in a time, and a mattering way of the community of all life.

Popper (1956/1983: 356, 358) did discount 'animistic belief' but he also critiqued logical positivism and logical empiricism as having 'similar anthropomorphisms' (p. 256) and his ironic standpoint was 'metaphysical realism'. We, by contrast, follow Gregory Cajete's (2000) *Native Science*, that declares that Western Science's dismissal of animism as anthropomorphic denies the IWOK in which everything, animate and inanimate, is connected by living energy, a position that is not so far removed from some kinds of quantum theory.

Western science with its linguistic turn, and with the Grounded Theory return to logical positivism, has turned natural laws into pseudo-statements, and, as such, Popper concludes 'that the question about their truth or falsity (is a pseudo-problem)' (Popper 1979/2014: 306 bracketed additions in original). Self-correcting induction is a demarcation of the problem being investigated that for Popper lies behind Wittgenstein's concept of meaning (p. 308). Popper's solution is the establishment of criterion that in a Kantian way bounds off natural science from metaphysics by writing out, demarcating and declaring '*a priori* propositions' (p. 308). Since the 'inductivist concept of meaning … is no more than shadow-boxing … becomes entangled in contradictions' and logical positivism is nothing but 'gross inconsistency' or a 'form of dogmatism' a new inductive method must be found (p. 323).

Still in New Zealand, Popper would have been teaching students about the error of logical positivism and how it played out in politics and society:

'During his time at the College he wrote and published *The Open Society and its Enemies*, comparing democracies founded on rational debate with authoritarian government. He went on to a position at the London School of Economics, and became a sought-after lecturer and speaker, attending conferences and debates around the world.'[3] Popper, like Peirce, had the standpoint that scientific knowledge advanced in an *evolutionary process*. Pierce had his triadic approach, and Popper (1973: 243) had his own formula:[4]

$$PS_1 \rightarrow TT_1 \rightarrow EE_1 \rightarrow PS_2$$

where:

PS$_1$ is response to a given problem situation

TT$_1$ is the number of competing conjectures, or tentative theories

EE$_1$ is error elimination similar to natural selection in biological evolution

PS$_2$ is theories that survive the refutation process to become applicable to the particular problem situation

After leaving New Zealand for London, Popper wrote *The Logic of Scientific Discovery* (1959) and *Conjectures and Refutations: The Growth of Scientific Knowledge* (1963). (An abandoned copy of this 1963 text had been left, probably by some other Erskine Fellows, in our University housing at the University of Canterbury. We mention this in case you noticed the ghost of Popper having a hand in writing this book.) As for Popper, 'He was knighted in 1965 and today is widely regarded as one of the greatest philosophers of twentieth century science'.[5] David thinks we should here and now amend that to read 'twenty-first century science'.

POPPER ON PLATO, HEGEL, AND MARX

Popper attacks the dialectics of Plato, Hegel, and Marx, by declaring that the future is open. Popper (1963: vii) is concerned how '*we can learn from our mistakes*'. His answer is we learn to do science by making guesses, anticipations about the future, or tentative conjectures which David calls 'antenarrative bets on the future'. Yet Popper must always engage in 'attempted refutations' applying Peirce's self-correcting induction to the two problems of knowledge (Popper 1979/2014) based on his research between 1930 and 1933, while being a *nay sayer* to the linguistic turn in the Vienna Circle. Finally, we in the English world have access to Popper's theory of falsifiability, and can unfold its role in *both/and (Big/little) storytelling science* and the entire Philosophy of Science.

Popper (1963) asserts that Plato's (428–348 BCE) dialogues oscillated between the pessimistic epistemology of *The Republic* and the optimistic epistemology of the *Meno*. It is in this oscillation that Plato defines induction. In Plato's *Republic*, several regimes cycle: (1) the first deviant regime from Kingship will be Timocracy with its pursuit of power, success and honor; (2) Oligarchy arises out of Timocracy by focusing on greed for wealth instead of honor; (3) As the rich become too rich and poor get poorer, there is a revolt favoring democracy's freedoms and equalities; (4) Desire becomes excessive, not just bodily desires but also desires for material goods, so Tyranny arises out of democracy. A tyrant is selected to be the champion of the people against the wealthy and against taxation, but eventually the people awaken from the con, and depose the lawless tyrant. The cycle goes back in search of the benevolent King or Queen.

Meno is a discourse about Socrates' dialogical questions to help the slave remember forgotten pre-natal knowledge their soul had possessed. Socrates' method is refutation by cross-examination. Socrates asks, 'can virtue be taught?' Socrates' focus is how philosophers talk a lot about virtue, but the people's focus is on wealth and power. Socrates gives the slave a geometry lesson, attempting to elicit the correct answer by asking leading questions, fishing for some remembered innate knowledge from the slave's past lives. Socrates attempts to make Meno aware of his own ignorance, and leads Meno to the correct answer by helping the slave think through deduction.

For Popper (1963: 12), Plato's dialogues are an invention of induction in several definitions. Popper is critical of Hegel's and Marx's dialectics. Throughout his writing, Popper makes scattered references to quantum physics and the Copenhagen Interpretation (he sided with Einstein rather than with Bohr). He also refers to Charles Sanders Peirce's work on inductive inference.

> Popper's falsifiability resembles Charles Peirce's nineteenth century fallibilism. In Of Clocks and Clouds (1966), Popper remarked that he wished he had known of Peirce's work earlier.[6]

Refutation (falsifiability) for Popper, and Peirce's fallibilism, are concepts central to what we are trying to do in *both/and (Big/little) storytelling science*. Both Popper and Peirce tried to develop inductive inference. For Popper:

> Inductive reasoning maintains that if a situation holds in all observed cases, then the situation holds in all cases. So, after completing a series of experiments that support the Third Law, and in the absence of any evidence to the contrary, one is justified in maintaining that the Law holds in all cases.[7]

This is a formulation similar to what we have reviewed in earlier chapters about Peirce's self-correcting induction method. Here is another tie between Popper and Peirce, with regards to quantum science (Popper 1972: 11):

> It seems to me that evolutionary processes or major evolutionary changes are as unpredictable as historical processes or major historical changes. I hold this view because I am strongly inclined towards an indeterminist view of the world, somewhat more radical than Heisenberg's: my indeterminism includes the thesis that even classical physics is indeterministic, and is thus more like that of Charles Sanders Peirce, or that of Alfred Landé.

POPPER ON INDUCTION

Karl Popper (1935/1959/1992/2000; 1963) offers several definitions of induction.

First Definition of Induction: *Reading Nature*

To infer from particular cases some universal laws of an entire population. Bacon calls this the True Method, making an interpretation of nature, and of the Universe, by reading nature as an Open Book. The True has to refute other 'Fake' interpretations that may be equally true, in order to get to what we are calling True Storytelling (Boje 2018d).

Second Definition of Induction: *Anticipation of the Mind*

To intuit or do sensemaking of the true nature of a thing, its '*veracitas nātūrae*' or 'truthfulness of nature' (Popper 1963: 7). This is an anticipation of the mind in Bacon's dualism of True Method and False 'Method of Induction'. Bacon's dualism of False and True induction asserts that judging a case in advance is to be avoided. As with Meno there is a search for non-manifest causes, by purging the soul of ignorance, and by purifying the intellect, purging all the false prejudices so that nothing else remains but 'unshakable basis of self-evident truth' (Popper 1963: 15). These are what Locke calls guesses, and Peirce terms intuited 'abductive-hypotheses'.

Third Definition of Induction: *Refutation of Conjectures*

Popper is not satisfied with these two definitions of induction, and adds his own. Popper is an advocate of the '*method of conjecture*' applied with refutations of what we call narratives with many counternarratives (or counter-instances). Popper (1935/1959/1992/2000: 2) says: 'Induction means finding singular events and from them deducing a general universal rule.'

Popper goes on to declare that given we can concoct an infinite number of these events to explain conjectures, induction is a weak epistemological tool, and any definite answer induction provides 'is going to be absurd' (p. 2):[8] 'In other words we have the choice of either an infinite regress or to postulate an a priori. To a serious thinker, that is like choosing between pest and cholera.' Popper's answer is to engage in refutations (falsifications) instead of trying to do verification. Peirce's answer is to combine induction-sampling of cases with abductive-hypothesis conjecturing and including deduction in a self-correction approach.

WHAT WOULD POPPER SAY ABOUT THE POSITIVE SCIENCE MOVEMENT?

The Positive Science movement, in its many forms of positive organizational scholarship (Cameron and Dutton 2003) has gained a strong foothold in many disciplines of the Academy of Management, from Appreciative Inquiry in the Organizational Development and Change Division and the Consultation division, to positive organizational behavior (OB) and positive leadership in the OB division. This optimistic epistemology has become its own regime of truth (Foucault 1984). For Popper (1963: 7), 'optimistic belief that truth and therefore goodness must prevail if and only if truth is given a fair chance' in free and open debate to expose and exorcise what we call 'Fake Storytelling' is a false ideology. An equally optimistic epistemology is the progress narrative, whereby we discern matters of truth by sensemaking, power of intellectual intuition, or by observation of nature. We think Popper would have the same skeptical view about the progress narrative idea that technology will save humanity from the unintended consequences of unsustainable practices (Boje 2019a; 2019c).

WHAT WOULD POPPER SAY TO THE NIHILISTS AND MARXISTS?

At the opposite extreme from Positive Science, the Academy of Management has vestiges of what Popper calls pessimistic epistemology. This is rooted in Schopenhauer's (1928) pessimism, his escape from science to artistic aesthetics, and in Nietzsche's (1968) 'will to truth', which is a 'will to power' to overcome nihilism, the meaninglessness of life in the sea of chaos. Popper would challenge the Critical Management Studies scholars (the Critters), and the Marxists and Nietzschean scholars, as practitioners of *pessimistic conspiracy* (grand) narratives. To the Marxist scholars, Popper (1963: 7) would say there is a 'conspiracy of a capitalist press that perverts and suppresses truth and fills worker's minds with false ideologies'.

WHAT WOULD POPPER SAY ABOUT THE WAVES OF GROUNDED THEORY?

Popper would say 1st Wave Grounded Theory has neither ground nor theory, and commits the most grievous 'inductive fallacy'. Grounded Theory inductive fallacy is defined as reducing ontology-of-Being to inductive-epistemological inference.[9] Figure 6.2 revisits the Grounded Theory figure presented previously.

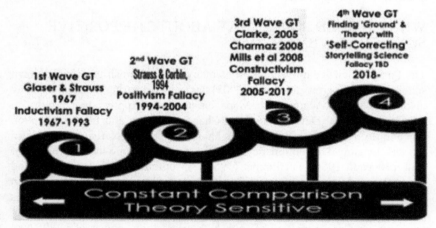

Figure 6.2   Four Waves of Grounded Theory (from Mark van der Klei, used with permission)

WHY DO THE FIRST THREE WAVES OF GROUNDED THEORY HAVE 'NO THEORY'?

By way of review: 1st Wave Grounded Theory is a what Popper (1963: 33) calls '*pseudo-science*', but even a 'pseudo-science may stumble on the truth'. 2nd Wave Grounded Theory has its '*empirical method*' which is also 'essentially *inductive*', but ends up being a 'pseudo-empirical method' (p. 33). 2nd Wave may have a lot of coding of observations, adding on diary notations as a practice of reflexivity, but there are no tests of refutation of the conjectures that would meet 'scientific standards' (p. 34). 3rd Wave Grounded Theory retreats into social constructivism, without the dialectical historical method of Berger and Luckmann (1967). Instead, 3rd Wave has rather a kind of sense-making of sensory observations without refutation.

In Grounded Theory's 1st, 2nd, and 3rd Waves there is a massive collection of empirical evidence, some by semi-structured interviews about *a priori* theme lists, others by observations of *etic* categories. There may be an occasional autoethnography, and/or scouring of archives of biographies for *a priori themes*. Yet in all, even with the exactness of measurability, and calculations of the number of stories and counterstories, and despite *verification* and *confirmation* of everything, something is missing. With this 'incessant stream of observations' all constantly verified by self and others' experience narratives, all that '*infinite regress*' (p. 43) of experience, we find not an ounce of refutation. It is for this reason, the all verification/confirmation without any refutation, that the 4th Wave, with its ontological turns to self-correcting induction (Boje 2019b), is a step towards an improved scientific method.

WHY DO THE FIRST THREE WAVES OF GROUNDED THEORY HAVE NO GROUND?

Inductive fallacy means reducing ontology-of-Being to inductive-epistemological inference. Our *both/and (Big/little) storytelling science* is ontological. It takes a self-correcting ontology to have ground. It takes self-correcting refutation of conjectures to have scientific theory, and a *both/and (Big/little) storytelling science*. Without self-correcting ontology Grounded Theory is groundless, and without refutation it is theory-less. In short, in the first three waves *there is no ground and no theory in Grounded Theory*. In Popper's (1963) *Conjectures and Refutations: The Growth of Scientific Knowledge*, Popper makes repeated reference to Peircean fallibilism, and there is one footnote #23, p. 240 to Volume 7, of Peirce's (1958) collected papers, specifically to paragraphs #182 and #206 that Popper (1963: 24) summarizes:

> In the search for a counter example, we have to use our background knowledge for we always try to refute first the *most risky* predictions, the '*most unlikely ...* consequences' (as Peirce already saw); which means that we always look in the *most probable kinds* of places for the *most probable* kinds of counter examples – most probable in the sense that we should expect to find them in the light of our background knowledge. Now if a theory stands up to many such tests, then, owing to the incorporation of the results of our tests into our background knowledge, there may be, after a time, no places left where (in the light of our new background knowledge) counter examples can with a high probability be expected to occur. (Peirce 1931–1935; 1958, italics original)

The eight volumes are available. This comes close to a self-correcting induction, which Peirce saw as a potential methodology to resolve the problem of inductive fallacy (Boje 2019b). It means to refute false storytelling rivals and counter examples of counternarratives, so there is a higher probability of finding 'True Storytelling' (Boje 2018d).

Next we conclude this chapter with yet more Peirce and Popper. Below, these two philosophers explain to us why we researchers, even we organizational storytelling researchers (and perhaps especially organizational storytelling researchers), are (or should be) all of us metaphysicians.

WE ARE ALL METAPHYSICIANS

Charles Sanders Peirce (1933–1937: 1.129) put it this way:

> Find a scientific man [or woman] who proposes to get along without any metaphysics – not by any means every man [and woman] who holds the ordinary reasoning of metaphysics in scorn – and you have found one whose doctrines are thoroughly vitiated by the crude and uncriticized metaphysics with which they are packed.

In short, we are all metaphysicians. We are metaphysicians doing what we will call '*storytelling science*' by critically questioning metaphysics, submitting metaphysics to what Peirce calls 'critical examination'. We are ontologists, and each ontology does a reduction to metaphysics. How does this reduction happen? Various '*ontologies*' reduce '*metaphysics*' by their preferred particular '*Occam's Razor*'. There are consequences of our ontological assumptions that limit our view of what we see as the purview of metaphysics. All this affects what we intend to study. Popper (1956/1983: 5) says he begins his classes on 'scientific method' by telling students: 'scientific method does not exist' and 'subject matter' does not exist, rather universities organize into a multiplicity of 'administrative' units whose *praxis* is 'the myth of the subject'. In sum, scientific method is even more non-existent than the 'non-existence of subjects' (ibid. p. 6). A paradigm is even more non-existent, as Popper (1994) later concludes in the book, *The Myth of the Framework*. Therefore, 'scientific method, and paradigm (Kuhn 1962) are not a way of finding scientific truth, nor another way to "*finding* a true theory"' (Popper 1956/1983: 6). And there is no *method* of finding a true story, and no *praxis* of finding an 'absolutely' true story. Rather 'scientific method' in *theory-method-praxis* consists of a '*kind of criticism*' with 'critical conversation' to refute or disconfirm the fake-stories, the 'fake-news', and the fake-frameworks, and the 'system of assumptions' and all the 'isms' such as 'positivism' and 'inductivism' used to justify the 'myth of the framework, itself' (Popper 1956/1983: 17). That is why Popper does 'critical metaphysics', testing conjecture after conjecture, that is a kind of self-correction to get a '*closer approximation to the truth*' by '*critically discussing*' to show what is '*not true*' (ibid., pp. 20, 23, 25).

Occam's Razor suggests we prefer a choice of theory which will give us the simplest explanation instead of a theory that gives us more complex explanations. Each reduction results in fallacy. In inductive fallacy, ontologies get reduced to epistemology, and ways of '*Being*' become mere ways of '*Knowing*' (Boje 2019b). Physics envy reduces all other sciences to rational/ nature ontology, the physics fallacy. Sociology can get reduced to psychology, and vice versa. Early anthropologists rejected indigenous metaphysics, and called it 'animism', and rejected animism in favor of WWOK. Gregory Cajete (2000) defends 'animism' as 'Native Science' in IWOK that comes from observing and revering Nature. Cajete talks about 'spiritual ecology' (Cajete 1993; 1994; 1999), about how every thing is living, spiritual, vibrant energy, and is interconnecting with everything else.

Positivism commits several fallacies. 'Logical positivism' is a double reduction of metaphysics to logical rationality, and to the positivism of confirmations without refutations. 'Logical empiricism' adds in metaphysics, only what is measured does actually exist. In business storytelling, all ethics can get reduced to instrumentalism, and so on. These are examples of reductions of '*metaphysics*'. We will assert such reductions to be 'storytelling science' and as such, each reduction is in need of various refutation tests. We will get to these. First, we turn to a deeper discussion of metaphysics.

A course in metaphysics is beyond the scope of this book, although David would love to include it. What we offer below is an outline for those wanting an overview of the field, and some direction on where to go to read more on various aspects of metaphysics most relevant to our topics here.

Metaphysics for Emmanuelle Kant (1785/1993: 1, #388) is twofold:

1. Metaphysics of Nature
2. Metaphysics of Morals

Kant's (1785/1993) review of classic Greek *sciences* is they are divided into three areas, but have an additional set of ontologies to reduce metaphysics with their particular reductionistic *Occam's Razors*. The three Science-Ontologies and their correct understanding of necessary subdivisions reduce one or both of the Kantian twofold metaphysics:

1. Physics, a science grounded on:
   a. Laws of Nature applied to differences of some Object
   b. Laws of Rationality.
2. Ethics, a science-grounded Universal Reason without regard to Object differences:
   a. Laws of Practical Freedom
   b. Laws of Morals.
3. Logic, a science grounded on Reason without an Empirical part.

Kant's storytelling of sciences and metaphysics is that three ontologies have emerged since the classic Greek era. In his historical reduction there are antecedent metaphysical roots which he does ignore.

4. Rational Philosophy:
   a. Material Philosophy grounded in understanding the Object
      i. Grounding on Laws of Nature
      ii. Grounding on Laws of Practical Freedom
   b. Grounded in understanding of Reason.
5. Natural Philosophy:
   a. Empirical part grounded in Experience
   b. Laws of Nature as Object of Experience.
6. Moral Philosophy grounded in Experience:
   a. Empirical part
   b. Laws of Morals.

This background sketch of metaphysics brings us to our subject area in management and organization studies. We propose a self-correcting abduction-induction-deduction semiotics, to get closer to approximations of 'true', knowing we are never arriving at 'absolute truth' because of our own fallibilism.

7. 'Industry remains in the greatest barbarism' (Kant 1785/1993: 2), one we contend is bringing us past tipping points of extinction (Boje 2019a; 2019b; 2019c).
   a. Empirical part is separated from the Rational part
   b. Empirical Physics preceded sometimes by a Metaphysical part
      i. Therefore a ground of obligation in the *a priori*
      ii. Therefore a ground of obligation in the practical Anthropology of experience.
8. Self-Correcting 'storytelling science' with several metaphysical variations of dialectic, anti-dialectic, dialogic, antidialogic, antenarrative, anti-narrative is available from these sources:
   a. Paulo Freire's (1970/2000) oppositions of dialectical and anti-dialectical with dialogical and anti-dialogical
   b. David Boje's (2011a) 'antenarrative' and 'anti-narrative' and colleagues' (Boje 2011a; Boje and Sanchez 2019a; 2019b; Jørgensen and Boje 2020) antenarrative and anti-narrative notions and implications for 'Quantum Storytelling' (Boje 2014; 2016a; Boje and Henderson 2014; Henderson and Boje 2016; Boje, Svane, and Gergerich 2016; Svane, Gergerich, and Boje 2017)
   c. Mikhail Bakhtin's (1981; 1990; 1993) anti-dialectical approach to several dialogisms (Boje 2008):

      i.   Polyphonic
     ii.   Stylistic
   iii.   Chronotopic
   iv.   Architectonic

d.   Charles Sanders Peirce's (1933-1937) 'self-correcting' semiotics of triadic of abduction-induction-deduction (Boje 2014)

e.   Gilles Deleuze's (1990; 1991; 1994; 1997; with Guattari 1987; 1994) anti-dialectics and retheorizing Bergson's (1960; 1988) multiplicities as assemblages of intensive, extensive and virtual multiplicities (Boje 2019b)

f.   Karl Popper's (2008) 'zigzag' of scientific method in the dialectical (*thesis-antithesis-synthesis*) problem solving to get closer to correct solution without falling into inductive fallacy in a moral ontology of middle ground between pessimism (Marxism) and optimism (positivism), and 'Metaphysical Realism'

g.   Henri Savall and colleagues' 'socio-economic' approach of dialectics (triadic of Peircean 'abduction-induction-deduction') and Qualimetrics (triadic of qualitative-quantitative-financial) in moral ontology of socially responsible capitalism (Savall et al. 2018; Boje 2018a)

h.   Hannah Arendt's (1978) series of dialectic cycles of *thesis-antithesis-synthesis* that become a spiral of self-correcting

i.   Jean Paul Sartre (1960/2004) dialectics of 'negation of the negation' in a practical ensemble of multiplicities as applied by Rosile, Boje, and Claw (2018) to Ensemble Leadership

j.   Judith Butler's dialectics of 'negation of the negation' as a way of undoing gender, and as applied by Riach, Rumens, and Tyler (2016) to Boje's (2001; 2008) 'antenarrative' and use of 'anti-narrative interviewing method' applied to Butler's (2005) giving account of oneself and (2004) undoing gender

k.   Slavoj Žižek's (2012) dialectics of 'negation of the negation' as a way to resurrect Hegelianism in relation to the Lacanian psychoanalytic.

HOW DOES THIS METAPHYSICAL ENSEMBLE WORK OUT IN 'STORYTELLING SCIENCE'?

We propose doing refutations to attain Popper's (1956/1983: xxv) 'metaphysical realism' by being critical of the stories, narratives, anti-narratives, and antenarratives of 'small s' 'storytelling science' and their relation to 'Grand Narratives' ('Master Narratives' and 'Petrified Narratives') of 'Big S' 'Science Narratives'. We give seminars at universities around the world to help dissertation (and thesis) students do what we are calling '*little s*' '*s*torytelling *s*cience'. Karl Popper (1956/1983: 13) was critical of 'Big *S*cience' with a 'capital *S*' because of his lifelong debates with 'Logical Positivism' of the Vienna Circle becoming the 'gospel of truth'. The Vienna Circle got its revenge on Popper by starting the myth that Popper was one of them, just one more logical positivist. Popper countered that he is a metaphysical realist, and subscribed to 'metaphysical realism' (Popper 1956/1983: xxv), described in a postscript to his first book in 1935 (*The Logic of Scientific Discovery*, which did not get translated from German to English until 1959).

As the story goes, Popper had to leave the German-speaking world and enter the English-speaking world, heading first to New Zealand, and then to the UK, in order to refute the myth of his logical positivism. As he wrote in his postscripts to his *Logic* book, Popper's '*metaphysical realism*' begins and ends with *fallibilism*, as does the work of Charles Sanders Peirce. Our purpose in writing this book is to show how the notion of *fallibilism* means that while truth is the self-correcting aim of 'little s' 'storytelling science', the best we can do is show that a theory-method-*praxis* is *not true* by the successive self-correcting tests:

1. Refutation test of *self-reflexivity conversations (autoethnography of your own living stories)*,
2. *Critical cross-disciplinary storytelling conversations with others to test and refute your own theory assumptions, abductive-hypotheses, assumptions of your inductive tests*,
3. *Understanding scalability processes of nature (and what various sciences say about your research question)*, 'for example, an area of the earth, together with its climate, hydrography, orography, flora and fauna, etc.' (Sartre 1960/2004: 43), and
4. *Doing experiments and practice interventions to get closer to solutions to super wicked problems such as the relations of the water cycle and the carbon cycle in global heating of the atmosphere since the industrial revolution, and how this is ushering in more and more crises which are larger and larger in scale and scope.*

We aim for the self-correcting 'storytelling science' to be seen as a continual process, undertaken in the humility of fallibilism. We never quite get to 'absolute truth' so we keep testing our own assumptions.

NOTES

1.   Online lecture notes 'Principles of Scientific Method' given at University of Otago 22–26 May 1945, accessed 8 March 2019 at http://popper-prior.nz/items/show/208.

2. Contents of an email from Andy Pratt, 8 March 2019: 'Eccles we talked about last night; Packer and Parton were chemists at UC, and Packer's son is also an academic chemist who retired to Christchurch (and, ironically, I have lunch with once a month …). I am pretty sure that this article was reprinted in a local chemistry rag, ChemNZ, in the 1990's but can't lay my hands on a copy at the moment.'
3. Artscentre.org/nz Karl Popper accessed 4 March 2019 at https://www.artscentre .org.nz/reflect/karl-popper/.
4. As cited, p. 35, in Philosophy and Rhetoric of Science, online text, accessed 7 March 2019 at https://s3.amazonaws.com/academia.edu.documents/ 31131563/philosophy_and_rhetoric_of_science.pdf?AWSAccessKeyId =AKIAIWOWYYGZ2Y53UL3A & Expires=1551895716 & Signature= jF0MM0HRmHWXfJ3b0BxOYV0McpU%3D&response-content-disposition= inline%3B%20filename%3DThe_logic_of_scientific_discovery.pdf#page=34.
5. Artcentre.org.nz, above note 3.
6. Philosophy and Rhetoric of Science, p. 35, accessed 7 March 2019 at https://s3 .amazonaws.com/academia.edu.documents/31131563/philosophy_and_rhetoric _of_science.pdf?AWSAccessKeyId=AKIAIWOWYYGZ2Y53UL3A&Expires =1551893106&Signature=ZsHhkcHkyyG5LvBE3ey3Jy3svAE%3D&response -content-disposition=inline%3B%20filename%3DThe_logic_of_scientific _discovery.pdf#page=53.
7. Philosophy and Rhetoric of Science, p. 9, accessed 7 March 2019 at https://s3 .amazonaws.com/academia.edu.documents/31131563/philosophy_and_rhetoric _of_science.pdf?AWSAccessKeyId=AKIAIWOWYYGZ2Y53UL3A&Expires =1551893106&Signature=ZsHhkcHkyyG5LvBE3ey3Jy3svAE%3D&response -content-disposition=inline%3B%20filename%3DThe_logic_of_scientific _discovery.pdf#page=53.
8. Citing from Popper's *Logic of Scientific Discovery*, online text, accessed 7 March 2019 at http://www.math.chalmers.se/~ulfp/Review/logicscdis.pdf.
9. My colleagues (Rohny Saylor, Marita Svane, and Yue Cai-Hillon) are proposing a 4th Wave of Grounded Theory that is thoroughly ontological.

7. Writing dialectical/dialogical and big/little storytelling science conclusions

In previous chapters, the especially deep and dense discussions of philosophy are usually sequestered into 'In Depth' sections. In Chapter 7 – did you guess from the title? – it is ALL deep and dense philosophy. We do have one 'In Depth' on Critical Metaphysics and Quantum Physics. The good news is that if you have read carefully thus far, you will be ready for Chapter 7 and parts of it will actually seem easy to read.

HOW TO DO DIALECTICAL AND DIALOGICAL IN A STORYTELLING DISSERTATION?

There are several dialectical logics used in *both/and (Big/little) storytelling science*. First we will begin with Aristotelian dialectic of syllogism and rhetoric. This dialectic is used primarily in narrative-counternarrative work. Second is the dialectics of Hegel, which Sartre calls Hegelian Dogmatism, and Popper also rejects. Many saddle Hegel with *thesis-antithesis-synthesis*, but in reading Hegel, he actually prefers the negation of the negation (Boje 2019b). It is the negation of the negation that Sartre, Heidegger, and Žižek attempt to rescue from Hegel (Boje 2019b). Third, we look at how Karl Popper develops a non-Hegelian, and non-Marxian *thesis-antithesis-synthesis*. He calls this the trial and error method of problem solving, cognizant of Peircean fallibilism, as more suitable to scientific inquiry. Fourth, we will look at the negation of the negation dialectic, and how it is used in the work of Jean Paul Sartre. This is especially important given our interest in ensembles of multiplicities, which are done differently than in Gilles Deleuze's writing.

ARISTOTLE'S SYLLOGISM AND RHETORICAL DIALECTIC

Aristotle in *Rhetoric* (I.1 book I, section 1) says: 'Rhetoric is the counterpart of Dialectic'. Aristotle reduced the 'Socratic Method', which was quite dialogical (Bakhtin 1981) then became reduced to the dialectical logic of Aristotle's 'Barbara' Syllogism (explained below). 'Furthermore, it is plain that it is the function of one and the same art to discern the real and the apparent means of persuasion, just as it is the function of dialectic to discern the real and the apparent syllogism' (Aristotle *Rhetoric* I.1). For Aristotle, rhetoric is an offshoot of dialectic and ethical studies. 'Neither rhetoric nor dialectic is the scientific study of any one separate subject: both are faculties for providing arguments' (*Rhetoric* I.2). In dialectic there is syllogistic logic on the one hand, and science on the other. He uses the language of 'premise', 'hypothesis', and the 'antithesis'.

The rhetoric of persuasion depends upon rhetorical syllogisms that include generally believable premises. Are conclusions drawn from premises? Can you draw conclusions from the results of previous syllogisms? The enthymeme (combination of minor premise and conclusion, as explained below) is given by Aristotle as an example of being an induction, with a few syllogistic propositions. Do the 'necessary' conclusions follow from the 'necessary' premises? Is the opponent's premise probable or not? 'Another good moment is when one premise of an argument is obviously true, and you can see that your opponent must say "yes" if you ask him whether the other is true' (*Rhetoric*, Book III.18).

In *Poetics* (#25), 'Things that sound contradictory should be examined by the same rules as in dialectical refutation whether the same thing is meant, in the same relation, and in the same sense. We should therefore solve the question by reference to what the poet says himself, or to what is tacitly assumed by a person of intelligence.' An enthymeme combines minor premise and conclusion, and the major premise gets implied. Aristotle's famous 'Barbara' Syllogism is widely studied. C. S. Peirce (1933–1937: 2.533), for example, says: 'Quite clearly, the Aristotelian syllogistic omits something', that there is a difference between teaching practical reason and analyzing reasoning in what cannot be false or mistaken. 'It is the argumentation or reasoning, not the logical form, which is dialectical' (1933–1937: 2.573). In this example, there is a major premise, minor premise, and conclusion, to which Peirce (2.570) would add the stricture of Rule, Case under the rule, and Result of the Rule. In this Barbara Syllogism the 'major premise' is implied that Socrates is mortal because he is a man (below adapted from Peirce 1933–1937: 5.328):

1. **Major premise (RULE)**: All men are mortal.
2. **Minor premise (CASE)**: Socrates is a man.
3. **Conclusion (RESULT)**: Socrates is mortal.

It may sound trivial, but it is easy to commit logical fallacy using syllogisms by making a deduction on false logic. Consider this next example:

1. **Major premise (RULE)**: All women like to shop.
2. **Minor premise (CASE)**: David likes to shop.
3. **Conclusion (RESULT)**: David is a woman.

Peirce's critique of the Barbara Syllogism is that it is demonstrative, mixing '*virtual*' with '*potential*' in a 'mechanical process' of interpretation that leads to fallacy, and his challenge is to the '*validity of the syllogism*'. The challenge is because the meaning of the major premise and the minor premise are different and do not necessarily oblige the conclusion (1933–1937: 5.328). Therefore the 'application of this corrective' of just 'mechanically reading the language of the syllogism' does not 'usually eradicate our sanguine disposition' (5.327).

POPPER'S REWORKING OF DIALECTIC INTO PROBLEM SOLVING

Popper's (1963: 320) adjustment to Aristotelian syllogism introduces the addition of 'some' to the classical theory (we have left Peirce's rule, case, and result format in play):

1. **Major premise (RULE)**: All men are mortal.
2. **Minor premise (CASE)**: Some Athenians are men.
3. **Conclusion (RESULT)**: Some Athenians are non-men.

Popper (1963: 312) also develops a shift in the 'dialectic triad: *thesis*, *antithesis*, and *synthesis*.' *Thesis* is an idea (theory or movement) that produces an opposition of the opposing (idea or movement) the *antithesis*. There is a struggle between *thesis* and *antithesis* we often see in narrative-counternarrative dialectic, but the third step, the *synthesis*, we find quite rare. More often the narrative thesis results in a struggle with many counternarratives (antitheses) and more antitheses are produced. Often further development to a synthesis stalls out or is gridlocked, as sometimes happens in two-party democracies. Popper's (1963: 314) solution is to toss out the ideologies, and focus on a 'trial and error', to get at an idea and its criticism. Popper attributes the triadic dialectic to Hegel's terminology of 'thesis and the antithesis' that 'by the synthesis' is '*negated*' (1963: 34, footnote #5). However, there is the other Hegelian dialectic, 'the negation of the negation' which is far more prominent in Hegel's work, and in fact Hegel was more often arguing against the dialectical triad. Marx picked up on the dialectical triad and made it into 'historical materialism' by eliminating the spiritual component (Boje 2019b).

SARTRE'S DIALECTIC LOGIC OF NEGATION OF THE NEGATION

Jean Paul Sartre's (1960/2004) *Critique of Dialectical Reason* develops a theory of practical ensembles of multiplicities. He focuses on the interplay between wholes (totalizations) and parts of ensemble multiplicities in relation to the whole.

> Such a logic of totalizations would be an abstract system of propositions concerning the multiplicity of possible relations of a whole to its parts and of different parts amongst themselves, either direct or mediated by their relation to the whole. (Sartre 1960/2004: 87)

Sartre's focus is the negation of the negation dialectic in these ensembles of multiplicities, which gets beyond the usual dichotomy of materialist and realist system and does not have the expectation some synthesis will develop out of an opposition or conflict:

> But this new process, the negation of the negation, derives its intelligibility, once again, from the original totality. In a realist and materialist system there can be no justification for asserting, *a priori*, that the negation of a negation must give rise to a new affirmation, as long as the type of reality in which these negations occur remains undefined. (Sartre 1960/2004: 89)

There are ensembles within ensembles arising within a totality, in which negation of the negation plays out:

> At all events, it is clear that the negation of a negation produces an indeterminate ensemble unless it is regarded as arising within a totality. But even within a totality the negation of the negation would be a return to the starting point if it did not involve a totality being transcended towards a totalizing end. (Sartre 1960/2004: 90)

The future is arriving in an oscillation of negation, transcended contradictions, and negation of the negation:

> Determination of the present by the future, oscillation between the inert and the organic, negation, transcended contradictions, negation of the negation – in short, developing totalization: these are the moments of *any* form of labour, until – at a dialectical level that we have yet to consider – society develops the division of labour to the point of the specialization of machines. (Sartre 1960/2004: 91, italics original)

Negation of the negation can work by diminishing scarcity and thereby relaxing alterity (the state of being different or Other). This fits the progress narrative of Western Ways of Knowing (WWOK), with its promise to increase the wealth of the community, but of course, wealth concentration appears to be the continuing result.

> The creation of a tool or an object of consumption diminishes scarcity – by a negation of the negation. It *ought* therefore, as such, to relax the tensions of alterity in the group, especially in so far as individual productive labour is also *social labour*,

that is, in so far as, whether individual or collective, it increases the wealth of the community. (Sartre 1960/2004: 151, italics original)

It is important for Appreciative Inquiry and all of the Positive Science movement to recognize that Sartre is looking at how the labor power of 'Others' is absorbed and turned back against everyone, in the interiorized scarcity of the negation of the negation, especially in late modern capitalism where there is much alienation as forms of corporate hierarchy displace more collaborative ensembles of multiplicities (Boje 2018c).

> At this level the real foundations of alienation appear: matter alienates in itself the action which works it, not because it is itself a force nor even because it is inertia, but because its inertia allows it to absorb the labor power of Others and turn it back against everyone. In the moment of passive negation, its interiorized scarcity makes everyone appear to Others as Other. (Sartre 1960/2004: 151)

In late modern capitalism, the worker is negated and materialized as a resource. Renditions of 'Human Resource Management' risk becoming a negation of the negation.

> The contradiction of the machine in the capitalist period is that it both creates and negates the worker; this contradiction is materialized into a general destiny and becomes a fundamental condition of the assumption of consciousness, that is to say, of the negation of the negation. (Sartre 1960/2004: 210)

Antenarrative constitutive praxis comes into play in the practical negation, and 'constitutes its destiny' in 'bets on the future'.

> … The praxis of the group, through the practical negation of its being-outside-itself as destiny, constitutes its destiny as future interest (through the material object), and as exigency contained in changing itself into interest-materiality. (Sartre 1960/2004: 210)

Today's new machines are digital, and they facilitate digital outcomes measures through surveillance in late modern capitalism. In this way, antenarrative digital forestructuring constitutes the 'destiny of the works as the *interest of the Other, controlling them in the form of counter-interest* (destiny)' in the social multiplicity. The struggle continues as wealth accumulates further among the already-wealthy.

> This is because the employers, by introducing new machines within the framework of capitalism and appropriating them *as their interest*, constitute the destiny of the workers as the *interest of the Other, controlling them in the form of counter-interest* (destiny), and because in the moment of social struggle, that is to say, of the *negation of the negation,* the real material objective can only be the negation of the

capitalist's interest in so far as it has become the worker's destiny, that is to say, the negation of the *interest of the other as negation.* (Sartre 1960/2004: 210, italics original)

Sartre builds up the ensemble of multiplicities in its reinteriorization of negation of the negation, constituted antenarratively in *praxis.*

It was only necessary to observe that synthetic self-determination is frequently the practical reinteriorization, as the negation of the negation, of the unity constituted by the other *praxis.* (Sartre 1960/2004: 362)

The ensemble of multiplicities applies to the nation-to-nation unit of analysis and to the organization-to-organization and group-to-group units of analysis. This allows a storytelling of the practical relation between the concrete organization and the developing entropy of disorganization:

It is true that this work is intended to replace a cloud of isolations (such as time-lags) by a functional unity; but in terms of the common praxis of organization, it shows that concrete organization is a perpetual negation of the negation, that is to say, a practical, effective negation of the developing disorganization. (Sartre 1960/2004: 545)

In sum, we have provided a presentation of how there are two kinds of dialectics, the dialectic triad of *thesis-antithesis-synthesis* and the negation of the negation (Hegel 1807/1977 does the latter type). It is the latter one that applies to the ensembles of multiplicities. In the next section we look at how the ensemble of multiplicities relates to Popper's and to Penrose's Three Worlds, and to Deleuzian multiplicities and Sartre's ensembles of multiplicities. If you are serious about doing *both/and (Big/little) storytelling science,* sorting out the antenarrative constituting processes of grander narratives and living stories is important to your dissertation.

We turn next to consider ensembles and multiplicities in greater depth. We begin with Sartre's 'ensembles of multiplicities' which we relate to Popper's Three Worlds and quantum physics (see Figure 7.1). We connect metaphysics in research with quantum physics. Finally, we conclude with a look at causation.

Sartre (1960/ 2004: 33) stresses: 'if there is such a thing as a dialectical reason, it is revealed and established in and through human *praxis*' in a place, in a time, by particular human activity, otherwise 'materialist dialectic will be meaningless' and 'can be *true* only within the limits of our social universe.' By contrast 'for the dialectic of Nature, it cannot be anything more than the object of a metaphysical hypothesis' (ibid., italics original). Logical Positivism has the 'provisional character of *dialectical hyper-empiricism*' forcing conclusions

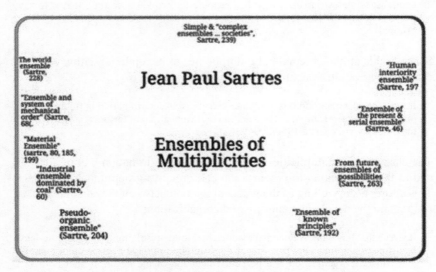

Figure 7.1   Some examples of Ensembles in Jean Paul Sartre

by the logic of the *a priori* (Sartre 1960/2004: 35). Sartre rejects the disguised spiritualism of the 'dialectic of Nature' (ibid.). Sartre begins constructing 'a multiplicity of totalizing individualities' defined as *dialectical nominalism*' (p. 37).

Next, we turn to Karl Popper and his theory of Three Worlds (see Figure 7.2), and then bring in Roger Penrose, after which we situate Sartre's ensembles.

We find it interesting and worth investigating that Popper's Three Worlds are the same as Roger Penrose's, but Penrose focuses on the relations between the worlds, and looks from the perspective of a quantum scientist at the three standpoints. Next, we situate our interest in Antenarrative Theory and Method into the Three Worlds. We added Ole Kirkeby's (2009) Platonic Greek Square to give some symbol of what is a Platonic World (see Figure 7.3). In this Platonic World, our freedom comes out of the dialogues of the True, the Just, the Beautiful, and the Good.

Now we are ready for Roger Penrose, whose quantum science is about the *between* of the Three Worlds (see Figure 7.4).

Clearly there is opportunity to do future research projects on the relation of Popper's Three Worlds and Penrose's and our own work on antenarrative standpoint. We did not forget about Deleuze.

We draw from Gilles Deleuze (1990; 1991; 1994) three multiplicities: the extensive relates to space, the intensive relates to time, and the virtual relates to mattering (see Figure 7.5). These constitute the 'between' relations of *both/*

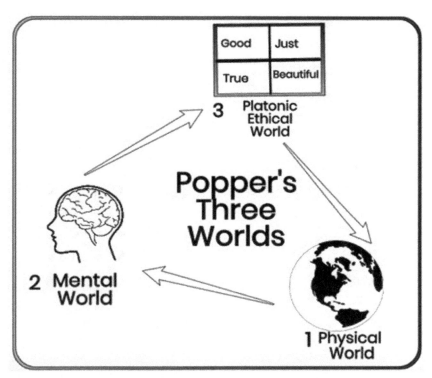

Figure 7.2   Popper's World 1 (Physical), World 2 (Mental), and World 3 (Platonic)

and (Big/little) storytelling science in our paradigm of the relational process ontology of Three Worlds. We find the Three Worlds developed in the works of Karl Popper (1978; 1972), in the triadic deduction-abduction-induction of Charles Sanders Peirce, and in Roger Penrose's (2011) work on Gödel, mind, and quantum physics. We have done some integration and related these Three Worlds to 'True Storytelling' through the work of Ole Kirkeby. We placed the constitutive processes of antenarrative in the center of the Three Worlds (see Boje 2019b).

Virtual mattering is the real, it is what we can see in Deleuze's (1990) deconstruction of the Robinson Crusoe story. It begins in a harsh world of black and white, without potentialities, suspended over the abyss, but progressively a revelation ascends out of the virtuality:

A harsh and black world, without potentialities or virtualities: the category of the possible has collapsed. Instead of relatively harmonious forms surging forth from,

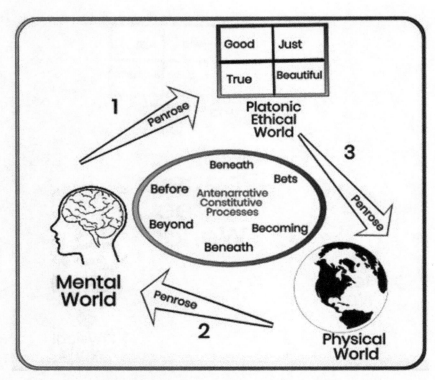

Figure 7.3   Antenarrative standpoint on the Three Worlds of Popper and a Kirkeby standpoint on Platonic World

and going back to, a background in accordance with an order of space and time, only abstract lines now exist, luminous and harmful – only a groundless abyss, rebellious and devouring. Nothing but Elements. The abyss and the abstract line have replaced the relief and the background. Everything is implacable. (Deleuze 1990: 305)

Thus Robinson progressively nears a revelation: initially he experienced the loss of Others as a fundamental disorder of the world; nothing subsisted but the opposition of light and night. Everything became harmful, and the world had lost its transitions and virtuality. But he discovers (slowly) that it is the Other who disturbs the world. The Other was the trouble. Having disappeared, it is no longer only the days which are redressed. Things are also no longer being pulled down by Others one on top of the other. (Deleuze 1990: 311)

We have examined assemblages of virtual objects with intensive and extensive multiplicities using Deleuzian ontology, and made some reference to Sartre's ensembles of multiplicity. This begs the question, what is the

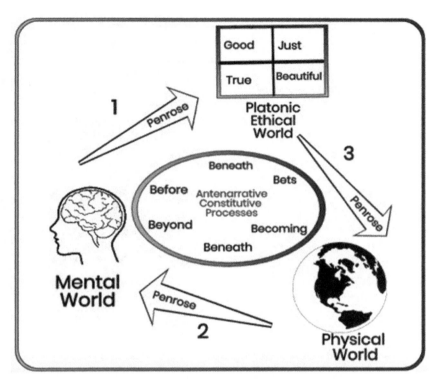

Figure 7.4   Penrose and Popper's Worlds have different standpoints

relation of Deleuzian multiplicities to the ensemble multiplicities of Sartre? In Figure 7.5, we placed Jean Paul Sartre's (1960/2004) notions of ensembles and their multiplicity. We want to map the relation of Gilles Deleuze's rhizomatic-assemblages of multiplicities (Extensive, Intensive, and Virtual Object) with those of Sartre. Sartre's standpoint seems to be looking in from 'ensembles of multiplicity' at the ways of testing hypotheses in experiment.

> We know the abstract conditions which this investigation must satisfy if it is to be possible. But these conditions leave its individual reality undetermined. In the same way, in the sciences of Nature we can have a general idea of the aim of an experiment (*expérience*) and the conditions for it to be valid, without knowing what physical fact is to be investigated, what instruments it will employ, or what experimental system it will identify and construct. In other words, a scientific hypothesis includes its own experimental requirements; it indicates, in broad outline, the conditions that the *proof* must satisfy; but this initial schema can be distinguished only formally from the conjecture which is to be tested. (Sartre 1960/2004: 62, italics original)

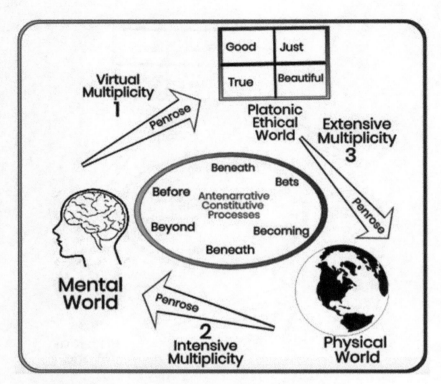

Figure 7.5   Deleuze's standpoint of the three multiplicities

For Sartre (1960/2004: 47–8, 51, italics original), 'the dialectic is a totalizing activity', a process of the ensemble of multiplicities that requires *critical investigation* upon anyone's 'reflexive experience' that becomes a moment in the process or a given region of reality, and how individuals are interiorizing the unique conditions of 'ensembles under consideration'. In this critical investigation, Sartre (1960/2004: 51–2) includes 'Alienation, the practico-inert, series, groups, classes, the components of History, labor, individual and communal *praxis*' in 'trying to establish the *Truth of History*'. By '*practico-inert*' we intend what Sartre defines as the 'alienated *praxis* and worked inertia' of the domain of equivalence' (p. 67). It is part of Dialectical Reason in the 'constituent and constituted reason of practical multiplicities' (p. 67).

In storytelling there are many particular articulations in the 'dialectic as the logic of creative action' that is a part of the 'logic of freedom' (ibid.). Here the Sartrean dialectic becomes an ensemble of multiplicities almost akin to Bakhtinian dialogisms, and both share practical multiplicity that can become dialogical or regress to enclaves of dialectical opposition. This calls into question any divide between dialogical and dialectical, at the level of ensembles of multiplicity, since in our theory of storytelling, both dialogical and dialectical processes are in the spontaneity of *praxis* which may devolve or evolve in synthetic and totalizing movement. For Sartre there are totalizing movements of ensembles of multiplicity, while for Deleuze the ensembles of multiplicity are rhizomatic.

It is in autoethnography that we re-live our 'membership of human ensembles with different structures and determine the reality of these ensembles through the bonds which constitute them and the practices which define them' and experience 'a living mediation between these different kinds of ensembles' in critical reflexivity (Sartre 1960/2004: 52). We can do critical reflexivity on the '*bond* between collectives and groups ... through the lived interconnection between affiliations' and 'through this disappearing *self*, grasp the dynamic relations between the different social structures' (ibid.). This is akin to 'Being in' the 'living story' ensembles of multiplicities, in the inseparability of *spacetimemattering* of *diachronic experience* and in the between of '*relations of interiority*' and the 'superposition of strata' and Deleuzian extensive multiplicity of cultural regions (p. 53). In short, from a Sartrean standpoint, this is dialectical investigation of diachronic evolution of ensembles of multiplicities, but from the Deleuzian standpoint it is the interplay of extensive, intensive, and virtual multiplicities that are rhizomatic. For Sartre, the 'social ensemble' becomes 'a particular avatar of *praxis*' and this is consistent with Deleuzian virtual multiplicities. The 'immediate, simple lived *praxis* ... in the course of time ... *discloses* itself, and progressively mediates itself through critical reflection' (Sartre 1960/2004: 56, italics original). Thus, the importance of 'reflexive critique' to 'reconstituting *praxis*' of the (auto) ethnographer (ibid.). In self-correcting, the ensemble of multiplicities 'establishes that the *bond of exteriority* (analytical and positivist reason) is itself *interiorized* by practical multiplicities, and that it acts within them (as a historical force) only to the extent that it becomes an interior negation of interiority, we will find ourselves situated, through the investigation itself, at the heart of a developing totalization' (Sartre 1960/2004: 57, italics original). Is this totalizing movement of dialectical reason intelligible to us? For us, the Dialectical Reason, to be constitutive, the totalization is projected beyond quantitative Peircean induction and qualitative induction through abductive-hypotheses, in a movement of self-correction of *both/and (Big/little) storytelling science* enterprise as *praxis*. For a Sartrean ensemble of multiplicities 'Interiority exteriorizes itself in order to interiorize exteriority' in the 'transparence of *praxis*' (Sartre 1960/2004: 60). In Savallian Qualimetrics there is the dialectics of the negated situation that enables the release of human potential in the inseparability of qualitative -quantitative-financial projects of practical *praxis* to reorganize the enterprise in socio-economic *praxis* of self-correction by successive experimentation (see Figure 7.6).

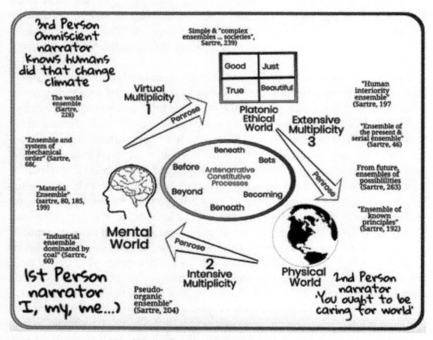

Figure 7.6   The Three Worlds of Popper, Penrose, Sartre and Deleuze

ENSEMBLES OF MULTIPLICITIES

Penrose (2011: 339) wants to make the multiplicities-connections between Three Worlds: quantum physics (Physical World), consciousness (Mental World), and Gödel mathematics (Platonic World). He looks from one world into another world, in a particular order. You may want two-way arrows, but that is not how Penrose makes his standpoint.

For the Platonic World we invoked the works of Ole Kirkeby (2000; 2008; 2009) and the Greek Square (see Boje 2019b for more on this). Mathematical entities are constructed mentally as beyond the minds of sensemaker's experience. Antecedent is the Physical World, with its laws of nature. Separating the Three Worlds of reality are three mysteries. Here we have placed them between the multiplicities of Gilles Deleuze (1990; 1991; 1994; 1997; Deleuze and Guattari 1987; 1994; see Boje and Saylors 2013; Boje 2019a; 2019b; Boundas 2010; Roffe 2010 for more). For Deleuzian multiplicities of multiplicities that are territorializing, deterritorializing, and reterritorializing in positive ensembles of extensive, intensive, and virtual multiplicities, we find storytelling part of the rhizomatic processes:

1. **Extensive Multiplicities**: Stories have spatializing-schema (*spatium*) spreading in the physical 'real' of interlocutor discourse. Story/narrative-schema in one part of the world are not the same schema as other story/narrative-schema or counternarrative-schema in another region. For example, freshwater may be stored differently in rivers, streams, or wells, from one region to another, and may taste different. Heterogeneous *spaces of varieties* of water are *mattering* differently in ice, vapor and liquid states, in bodies of glacial water, lake, river, ocean, artesian springs, aquifer groundwater, and in all living bodies as *élan vital* (life force). Real water is consumed in all phases of production, distribution, and consumption in the *spacetimemattering* (Barad 2007) of 'Water Capitalism' (Boje 2019a).
2. **Intensive Multiplicities** of **heterogeneous times of water duration** (*dureé*) include the mattering of water-now-past, water-now-present, and water-not-yet. Stories have different temporal horizons: Coca-Cola has a quarterly report time horizon; the farmer's horizon is seasonal. Water-replenishment in one kind of aquifer can take years, but in another it takes centuries or millennia. It is artificial to separate spatializing from temporalizing, and these from mattering.
3. **Virtual Multiplicities**: In Deleuze and Guattari (1987) there are fractal calculations. Now we have the virtual object of water calculations (Boje 2019c). Water is direct use, and many times that volume is involved in production and distribution processes of a global corporate supply chain. Water is a 'virtual object' when water calculations are missing or hidden inside the process that is used to make fuel for machines, or is hidden in manufacturing and transportation processes. It has been calculated that several liters of 'virtual water' go into making a single-use plastic or glass bottle. Water undergoes 'virtual object' transformation when water is used to erect concrete walls, and maintain a multi-million dollar bottling plant, and so on.

Thus we see there are many varieties of multiplicities. Now add to this the concept of an 'assemblage' of multiplicities, where 'assemblage' refers to an unorganized or loosely organized group. Gilles Deleuze (1994: 239) makes it clear the issue is not about dualizing qualitative and quantitative when it comes to dynamics of assemblages of multiplicities.

> In short, there would no more be qualitative differences or differences in kind than there would be quantitative differences or differences of degree, if intensity were not capable of constituting the former in qualities and the latter in extensity, even at the risk of appearing to extinguish itself in both.

Deleuze (1994: 239) found Bergson's notion of intensiveness unconvincing as an explanation of multiplicity dynamics: 'It assumes qualities ready-made and extensities already constituted. It distributes difference into differences in kind in the case of qualities and differences in degree in the case of extensity.' The problem for storytelling is quality gets attributed to schemata extensivity, or it becomes a superficial movement of a mixture of qualitative and intensive multiplicities. Deleuze's (1994: 239) solution is to:

> Define qualitative duration not as indivisible but as that which changes its nature in dividing, that which does not cease to divide and change its nature: virtual multiplicity, he says, in opposition to the actual multiplicities of number and extensity which retain only differences of degree.

Sartre's solution to multiplicity dynamics focuses on 'practical ensembles' of multiplicities, in a 'negation of negation' dialectic that, of course, Deleuze would not endorse. Deleuze and Sartre's approaches to multiplicity are both about totalizing assemblages, but their theorizing is vastly different. It is a topic for many future dissertations.

Karl Popper (1972; 1978) gives his three-world rendition, which in many ways parallels or anticipates the Three Worlds of Penrose (2011). In Popper's (1978) lecture, like Peirce and Penrose, he challenges the monadic (one world) view, and the dualistic (two world) view with Three Worlds:

World 1 'consists of physical bodies: of stones and of stars; of plants and of animals; but also of radiation, and of other forms of physical energy' (Popper 1978: 142). Like Penrose, he calls this the 'Physical World'. He divides World 1 into living and non-living things. In Popper's view (1972: 153), his theory is a pluralism thesis of the Three Worlds.

World 2 consists of 'mental or psychological ... our feelings of pain and of pleasure, of our thoughts, of our decisions, of our perception and our observations; in other words, the world of mental or psychological states or processes, or of subjective experience' (Popper 1978: 143). This world can be subdivided into conscious experiences from dreams, and subconscious experiences. We WWOKers can also distinguish between animal and human consciousness (Popper 1978 143).

World 3 is composed of 'products of the human mind, such as languages; tales and stories and religious myths; scientific conjectures or theories, and mathematical constructions; songs and symphonies; paintings and sculptures' (Popper 1978: 144). World 1 and World 3 share many of the same things, such as Michelangelo's sculptures, his Codex, and Shakespeare's works, even the Bible, and Beethoven's Fifth Symphony, and Newton's theory of gravitation. These things (objects) are embodied in World 1 by art galleries, orchestras, and theater performance companies (Boje 2017a). In World 3 they are virtual (abstract objects). Popper (1972: 153) includes Plato's world of Forms or Ideas, the Stoics, and Frege, Leibniz, and Bolzano, but not Hegel who he rejects for his monistic tendencies. He adds, 'Platoism goes beyond the dualism of body and of mind' (p. 154).

Popper's point is the dualist accepts both the World 1 materialism and the World 2 experience of 'remembering as real' the *experience* of listening to Beethoven's Fifth Symphony (Popper 1978: 147). In the critical realism of evaluation of works of art, there is the work, the embodiment of the work, and some objectivist view of its greatness, that has a causal effect in World 3 and on World 2 and what is considered an object in World 1. Popper says, 'I am a realist regarding' World 3 – the World 3 'that consists of abstract objects, such as languages; scientific conjectures or theories; add "works of art" and the "three fold realism" of all three worlds' (Popper 1978: 151).

Let us turn to the writing of the conclusion of research as it addresses findings of causality. Popper (1972: 155) addresses causal relations between the Three Worlds, with the World 2 acting as mediator between the World 1 and World 2. 'It cannot be denied that the World 3 of mathematical and scientific theories exerts an immense influence upon' World 1 (p. 155). Unlike the behaviorists, Popper supports the thesis of World 2: 'a subjective mental world of personal experiences exists' (p. 156).

At heart, Popper is ever the linguist, focused on argumentative inquiries, assertions, admonitions, prayers, and narration but is able to treat World 3 as a man-made product (Popper 1972: 158). He goes on to emphasize that the World 3 world is 'not a fiction but exists "in reality"' and has a 'tremendous effect on World 1, mediated through' World 2 (Popper 1972: 159). As we depicted, Peirce (1931/1960) treats Thirdness (induction) as mediating Firstness (abduction) and Secondness (deduction), and like Popper, Peirce is working out ways to shore up induction, and both have their tests of self-correction. Both Popper and Peirce develop induction in relation to hypothesis and deduction, but Peirce prefers abduction (retroduction) instead of a direct hypothesis.

For us, *both/and (Big/little) storytelling science* has been done poorly as a mechanistic search for cause and effect framework. This has degraded storytelling sensemaking. 'Quantum Storytelling' is not mechanistic causalism, but rather it is an organic and dynamic interpretation and meaning of 'quanta forces'. Popper (1956/1983) does various critiques of the quantum theories of Bohr, Heisenberg, Bohn, Schrödinger, and Einstein concerning the Copenhagen Interpretations and various counternarrative explanations of results of the double slit experiment.

Karl Popper's (1956/1983: 132) 'metaphysical realism' begins with 'Each of the statements' about a 'state of affairs' he calls the '*explicandum*' and asserts the aim of science is problem solving, to find '*satisfactory explanations* of whatever strikes us as being in need of explanation'. This he terms the '*explicans*' that are the discovery of '*the explanation of the known by the unknown*'. Popper (1956/1983: 445) is critical of Neils Bohr's interpretation for 'smearing of the *frame of reference*' of the measurement of position in

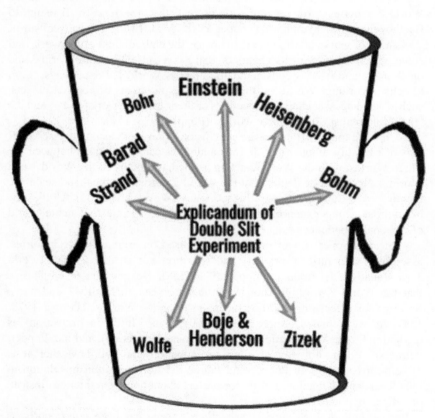

Figure 7.7　　*Quantum Storytelling interpretations of the explicandum of the double slit experiments*

space and the measurement of momentum in space in the complementarity principle. Popper is equally critical of Werner Heisenberg's 'uncertainty principle' that subordinates the physical (World 1) to the math calculations (World 3). Popper finds David Bohm's explanation of the double slit experiment results unsatisfactory. Popper is more sympathetic to Einstein's objection to the 'dice-playing god' (Popper 1956/1983: 400) than with Bohr's principle of complementarity and Heisenberg's principle of indeterminacy, different Copenhagen Interpretations. In Figure 7.7, we have included Barad (2007) and Strand (2012) who side with Bohr against Heisenberg, and Žižek (2012), who has a Hegelian 'negation of the negation' dialectical critique of Barad's *agential realism* theory of the intra-activity of materiality *with discourse*, for not allowing the 'dash' ('-') between intra and activity to denote a dialectical relationship between these terms. We also include Wolfe (1988), who, like Žižek, has a role for the spiritual in quantum science, as do Boje and Henderson (2014).

In Depth: Critical Metaphysics and Quantum Physics

The mattering theories of quantum physics have always contained some very metaphysical assumptions. Popper (1956/1982: 162–72) gives his metaphysical realist critique:

1. **Parmenides** – the world is full of matter and the void of emptiness cannot exist.
2. **Democratis** – Atomism means the world is not full of matter, and there are empty voids so atoms can move and rearrange.
3. **Plato** – The physical world is space filled by matter.
4. **Aristotle** – Space is matter (extensive substance), the body in dualism, with form, its essence (essentialism) and therefore the final cause is the potentiality of matter.
5. **Descartes** – The potentiality of matter (body extension) and its dualistic relation to mind.
6. **Hobbes and Descartes** – Matter is the clockwork machine in its spatial extension, with Aristotelian 'action at a distance'.
7. **Kant** – Following Newton, the push and attraction forces explain causation, and matter is space filled by repulsive forces.
8. **Faraday and Maxwell** – Fields of forces, vectoral forces with local changes at vanishing distances as atoms (or molecules) inhabit the force field.
9. **Einstein and Schrödinger** – The unified force field theory refutes the theory of clockwork cosmology (materialism). Schrödinger theory of wave packets.

10. **Heisenberg** – Copenhagen Interpretation of double slit experiment, as the Principle of Indeterminacy (aka Uncertainty) by doing a statistical matrix of how particles probably behave when there is the observer effect. Popper calls this the 'end-of-the-road' thesis. The last revolution of theory in quantum physics would mean 'end of history', which Popper refutes.
11. **Bohr** – Copenhagen Interpretation of double slit experiment, as the Principle of Complementarity. Popper calls this another 'end-of-the-road' thesis, which Popper also refutes. Popper's refutation is that Bohr has a non-realist position.
12. **Einstein-Podolsky-Rosen (EPR)** – Rejects 'end-of-the-road' of quantum physics, and has a thought experiment that more theories are possible to refute Copenhagen Interpretations. There may be a layer of physical reality deeper than what is represented in the overlaying Copenhagen Interpretations. EPR theory states that a particle cannot have a sharp position and momentum at the same time.
13. **Bohm** – David Bohm amends EPR with a theory of polarity of spin that is experimentally testable.
14. **Popper** – Proposes additional experiments to test the double slit interpretations, in possible refutation of end-of-the-road interpretations, citing the new particles being discovered, such as the meson and neutrino. Supports EPR theory of the threshold of quantum waves.

Popper (1956/1982: 10) asserts that these quantum theories have metaphysical assumptions and that 'quantum mechanics is not a description of reality'. In sum, metaphysical speculation plays its role in quantum theories, and the process of more quantum theories refuting or challenging aspects and assumptions of older theories continues. Popper (1956/1982: 31) recommends a 'metaphysical research program' be part of the 'course of scientific research and development'. Metaphysics and science can focus on the problem situation. Popper has dreams of the 'metaphysical' (p. 198). He is all about 'metaphysical realism'.

There is a nihilist trait in multinational corporations and academies subverting 'little s' 'storytelling science' into a mechanistic cause and effect duality. This mechanistic approach frames the calculability of events into mathematical formulas that appear objectively quantified but are fiction and illusion. We agree with Sartre (1960/2004: 65) that the agreement between '*praxis*' and 'self-conscious' reflexivity can become *praxis-process* or 'incarnations of *praxis*' in '*series*' and 'transition from series to groups and from groups to series as constant incarnations of our practical multiplicity, and to test the dialectical intelligibility of these reversible processes'. This is a statement of a Sartrean ensemble of multiplicity of self-correcting induction that includes Testing, Knowing, Being, and Doing in a critical intelligibility of *praxis*, which we theorize as constituted by antenarrative processes antecedent to story and narrative.

WHAT IS CAUSALISM?

For Nietzsche (1968:#554 p. 300) *'causalism'* is defined as 'things-in-themselves cannot be related to one another as cause and effect, nor can appearance be so related to appearance; from which it follows that in a philosophy that believes in things-in-themselves and appearances the concept "cause and effect" *cannot be applied*' and is Kant's biggest mistake. Heidegger (1927/1962) calls it an ontic fallacy. For Peirce (1931/1960), it is a reduction of ontology to epistemology. Nietzsche (1968: #551 p. 295) in his *'Critique of the concept of "cause"'* concludes: 'There is no such thing as cause', 'There is neither causes nor effects', 'Event is neither effected nor does it effect', and 'Interpretation by causality [is] a deception'. He rejects Aristotle's fourfold cause as a fiction, a fear of chance, and an uncertainty due to dynamic forces that are organic, not mechanistic. Storytelling attributes *'causa efficens'* and *'causa finalis'* (ibid.). 'We intuit causes after the scheme of the effect' *post hoc* (ibid.). That is why self-correcting induction method is so very important in 4th Wave Grounded Theory. Causalism is a psychological storytelling belief and a judgment *post hoc* that when observing one event following another event we can interpret cause and effect and 'that every event is a deed' and presupposes a 'doer and action-subject'. For Nietzsche, this is the 'great stupidity' of mechanistic thinking (ibid.). 'The law of causality has been projected on to every event' (ibid.: 296). The storyteller projects the cause and tells how it happened and who got it to happen. Some event must be responsible that some doer intended.

In the Quantum Storytelling paradigm shift, 'thing-in-itself' and 'subject-in-itself', that great duality of cause and effect in mechanistic science, disappears, and the dynamic 'complexity of events' in its organic ensemble of multiplicities becomes possible to interpret (Nietzsche 1968: #552, p. 298). We conclude that will to power and will to truth are related to what we have discussed as the relation of 'Quantum Storytelling Theory' to 'True Storytelling *praxis*.' According to Nietzsche (1968: #552, p. 298):

> Will to truth is making firm, a making true and durable, an abolition of the false character of things, a reinterpretation of it into beings. 'Truth' is therefore not something there, that might be found or discovered – but something that must be created and that gives a name to a process, or rather to a will to overcome that has in itself no end – introducing truth, as a *processus in infinitum*, an active determining – not a becoming-conscious of something that is in itself firm and determined. It is a word for the "will to power"'. (Ibid.)

This 'will to power' is not mechanistic cause and effect, but rather the relations of dynamic forces that stem from a 'will to truth'.

PHILOSOPHERS AND QUANTUM SCIENTISTS

Knowing (or epistemology), Being (or ontology), Self-Correcting (methodology), and doing (or *praxis*) was summed up by Frank Sinatra, Do-Be-Do-Be-Do, as an iterative process (see Figure 7.8). We could add Do-Be-Test-Be-Do, but that does not have the same ring to it. From Jean Paul Sartre (1960/2004) we give a few examples of his practical ensembles, which we find relevant to the work on ensembles of multiplicities (Rosile, Boje, and Claw 2018).

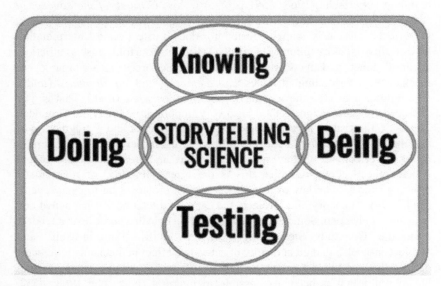

Figure 7.8   Knowing, being, self-correcting, and doing

Both Popper and the quantum scientists such as Roger Penrose theorized Three Worlds, as a way to get beyond the 'one-world monologic', and Cartesian dualism of two world either/or logics. This Triadic, the Three Worlds of Ensembles of Multiplicity, we find also in Charles Sanders Peirce. We connect some of Jean Paul Sartre's three-world relations to that of Popper, and bring in the multiplicities of both Gilles Deleuze and Jean Paul Sartre.

What is our conclusion? It takes successive Knowing, Being, Testing, and Doing to have a *both/and (Big/little) storytelling science* dissertation (see Figure 7.9). Collapsing Knowing into Being is the ultimate inductive fallacy. Collapsing 'Knowing' and 'Being' into 'Testing' is positivism. Not Testing

Figure 7.9   We conclude with these philosophers and scientists

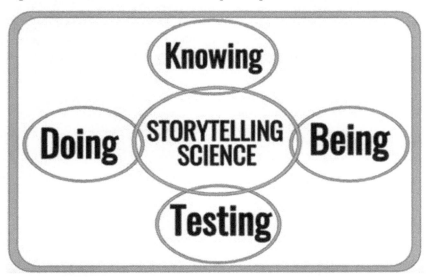

Figure 7.10   The knowing, being, testing, doing iterations of a both/and (big/little) storytelling science dissertation

'Knowing, Being, and Doing' is Positive Science. In *both/and (Big/little) storytelling science* is the inseparability of Knowing, Being, Testing, and Doing we find in the work of Savall, Sartre, Peirce, and Popper (see Figure 7.10).

Writing a good *both/and (Big/little) storytelling science* conclusion includes your contributions of Knowing, Being, Testing, and Doing, plus your limitations and future research statements. These are your antenarrative bets on the future. These are your premises related to your conclusions.

EXERCISE 7.1   POSITION YOUR RESEARCH IN RELATION TO METAPHYSICS AND QUANTUM PHYSICS

Question 1: Quantumness is about connectedness and entanglements, and for some, this connectedness can be metaphysical, but not necessarily religious. Most of us have had, or know someone who has had, what some would consider 'strange' experiences relating to this connectedness. Grace Ann dreamed her sister was crying, and the next day, found out her sister had discovered a lump in her neck the night before and was sobbing in panic. Some have said they prayed and God spoke to them, and the next day, what the divine message predicted showed up in their lives. Some people 'just had a feeling' and avoided a place where they later found out a terrible accident had happened. Scientists report breakthroughs due to a 'hunch', which we relate to the abductive process. **SHARE WITH A PARTNER:** Tell the story of a time in your life, or the life of someone you know, where you have seen or experienced this sort of connection. Is this relevant to your research?

Question 2: **SHARE WITH A PARTNER**: We quote Popper's comment that 'There is no scientific method.' In the 'Method' section of an upcoming or past research paper, how would you defend your research method and respond to Popper?

8. Managing the oral examination and post-submission process

David had his oral examination for his dissertation at the University of Illinois in 1978. He presented the first sentence to explain his dissertation, and he was cut off. Faculty on the committee and faculty in the gallery argued for over 90 minutes, and then decided, given that time was running out, to pass him, despite everyone's unsettled reservations. David was somewhat shaken by the process, but he decided that letting them argue was wiser than adding fuel to the fire. Usually an oral examination sets aside 30 minutes or so for the doctoral candidate to present their thesis, its research question, some brief literature review, some methodological approaches, findings, conclusions, limitations, and some future research prospects.

The oral exam and post-submission process varies internationally. In some countries, down under, and in Europe, the committee members help the student get to the defense stage, then the final decision is given over to external evaluators. Often at least one of them is from another country. They are blind evaluators, in that mostly they have not met the student, and never worked with them on their research. This is a risky process, full of chance and egoism. Choosing an external whose research is not cited, is an especially risky course of action. Choosing a 'name' in the field has the risk that the candidate presumes to know more than the 'name'. Choosing a newer full professor, whose ears are still ringing from the challenges of their own oral exam, is also risky.

When David was on the other side of the fence and an examiner rather than a candidate, he had an unusual experience. It was about a decade ago, and David had been well established for many years, and he was brought in to be a 'judge'. Two external reviewers, from two different countries, were in disagreement. The University asked David to break the stand-off by making the final decision. Either decision would offend two well-known 'names' in the field of the dissertation. Perhaps David was the only one dumb enough to accept the judgeship. David found in favor of the student, and against the external reviewer who had elected to completely reject the dissertation. He voted in favor of the external examiner who concluded the dissertation was a path-breaking and brilliant contribution to the field. By the way, the student had not cited either examiner in the literature review. The Goddess Fortuna played a trick on David and the two external examiners. It happened at a well-funded seminar that included the two examiner characters in this story, but not the now passed candidate who did receive their PhD. As with most storytelling of note (which ironically tends to occur in the coffee line or during a break), it went like this.

> External #1: 'David, I was external on a dissertation on X, and it was marvelous, one of the best I have ever been asked to examine. Then all hell broke loose'.

Two minutes later, David returned to the line for another chocolate cookie (they were small).

> External # 2: 'David, I was external on a dissertation on X, and it was the most god-awful thing I ever read. So I rejected it outright. What is the world coming to?'

David did some soul searching. What is the right thing to do? The process is supposed to be blind, anonymous, and the identity of any externals who are in dispute, as well as the judge, are never to be disclosed. Still there is a moral obligation here, to learn, to bring disputants into dialogue, to learn to do better. David goes to each external:

> David to External #1: 'I have a problem. I was the external for the aesthetics dissertation at Y University. And the other external you disagreed with happens to be here. Would you like to meet up, and discuss the events?'
> External #1: 'Yes I would like that'.
> David to External #2: 'I have a problem. I was the external for the dissertation on X at the Y University. And the other external you disagreed with happens to be here. Would you like to meet up, and discuss the events? The other examiner has already agreed'.
> External #2: 'Yes, let's meet up here and now'.

So they sit off in a corner during the rest of the break.

> David: 'Thanks for agreeing to meet each other. I really respect each of you. It was a difficult decision to support one of you and risk offending the other. I don't much like the process of having externals come in after the fact, to evaluate a dissertation. It takes away sovereignty and it's colonialist empire at its worst'.
> External #2: 'No worries David, we're still friends. I know you were doing what was right, between a rock and a hard place.'
> External #1: 'We can talk about X-related theories later. I agree, the process of external reviews leaves a lot to be desired. How did academia get in such a mess?'
> David: 'I don't know. I know in the US, there is an external to the committee from another department or college, but they are there to ensure fairness and that University policies are followed. Usually they are an observer, an advocate for due process, but do chime in with questions. Then the committee votes up or down. In Nordic countries, and down under, if an external votes it down, it can be the end, and a student gets the consolation prize of a master's degree, or nothing'.

EXERCISE 8.1   MANAGING THE ORAL EXAM

In advance of your exams, PRACTICE with everyone you can find. Use fellow students regardless of their discipline, as long as they can spare a half-hour to hear your short presentation (time yourself!) and ask questions and give you some feedback. Use your relatives too. Be sure you have good visuals, overheads and/or handouts.

Similar to your rounds of self-correcting at the research stage, you should be giving your chapters as they are completed to your committee chair as you go along, to allow for course corrections along the way. Some readers may prefer to see the whole document at once, and we have seen documents that were best read that way. However, if your chair will read and give feedback as you go, we feel that is the best way to proceed.

Be concise, avoid digressions, and focus on your most exciting parts.

Ideally, you will have committee members who do not have grudges among themselves. If they do, it is best to do as David did, let them talk it out among themselves. Ideally, your committee chair will be the strongest academic on your committee. If not, try to consult with all committee members before the defense, but only if your chair agrees to this.

The following exercise can help you to prepare for the actual defense.

PART 1

Choose a partner. Decide who will be Partner A and who will be Partner B.

Take two minutes to think about your answers to the questions below.

Then Partner B go first with your answers for two minutes, then Partner A for two minutes.

Conclude with two minutes to discuss similarities and differences.

Next, move to Round 2 (questions are below).

This time, Partner A goes first answering the questions for two minutes, then Partner B answers for two minutes.

PART 2

Then, in Part 2, you will repeat the process with different questions and a different time frame. In Part 2, you will imagine yourself five years in the future. You meet a former classmate by chance at an airport while you are waiting for a plane. You have not seen each other since you each had your (successful) defenses. Each partner, take two minutes to tell the other what happened at your IDEAL defense. Remember – you will be describing the ideal future you WANT to have happen.

(Six minutes, longer if you wish) Part 1 QUESTIONS:

(Two minutes for Partner B, then two minutes for Partner A, then two minutes to discuss together)

1. **Before you began your PhD program, what did you think it would be like?**
2. **What was different or unexpected about it?**

TOGETHER, discuss similarities and differences.

(Six minutes, longer if you wish) Part 2 QUESTIONS:

(Two minutes for Partner A first, then two minutes for Partner B, then two minutes to discuss together)

1. **What happened at your very successful defense? What was the best part?**
2. **What wonderful things have happened over these five years as a result of your successful defense?**

TOGETHER, discuss similarities and differences.

In case you would like some examples to get you started, following are Grace Ann and David's answers to the Part 1 questions.

Grace Ann's answers: Different and unexpected? I had an image that a PhD was a person who spent a lot of time quietly reading and thinking deep thoughts in a book-lined office. I quickly learned that life as a PhD student was incredibly busy, and most reading was done while burning the midnight oil, or sitting in a hallway speed-reading a forgotten assignment in the hour before class. But it was not all work overload. I had some of the best times of my life with my fellow students informally discussing weighty philosophical issues. I respected and admired my classmates, and I felt fortunate to be in their company.

David's answers: What I thought the PhD would be like? I was in the MBA program and had only finance courses left. I was bored by finance. So I took a couple of PhD seminars in organizational behavior as electives. As an MBA student I thought I would have trouble keeping up with the PhD students in OB. But to my surprise, I loved every moment of it. It was different to challenge the theories instead of just memorizing them for tests. I also began to see how theories were crafted. I did pretty well. The professors of the department invited me to apply for the PhD. They were horrified at my low GMATs. You see I had been kicked out of high school English, Typing, and a few other classes. Anyway, I was admitted.

What was unexpected in the PhD? The focus on statistics, and multivariate analysis. There were theory classes, then we went straight to doing surveys and lab experiments. But then toward the end of the program, Lou Pondy, decided to take a sabbatical and study cultural anthropology. He mentored me about storytelling, and its sociological role. The other thing unexpected was I had to become a teacher instantly. Being a TA was how people were funded. After a semester of trying to do experiential teaching of a management class, Lou Pondy, asked me to be an assistant coordinator for 14 sections. He liked my approach to treating the classroom as a learning organization, and dividing the class into departments complete with managers. It was new in those days, and we called it the 'Experiential Learning Organization' (ELO). That meant training other doctoral students and a few adjuncts in how to teach experientially.

NOTE: We refer you to the Exercise 5.1 for advice on continuing your research and managing your academic career post-dissertation-defense.

FINAL WORDS

Conversational storytelling interviewing and self-correction (Abductive-Inductive-Deductive) go hand in hand. Together, they make 'storytelling science' a rigorous research method. Together, they provide a way to use refutation to challenge conjectures, to be both dialogical and dialectical as the situation demands. Most of all, storytelling conversational interviewing is both exploratory and a way to zigzag between conjecture and refutation. In sequential rounds we get closer to producing something fun and interesting.

Life would be pretty dull without the unexpected things. Sometimes the unexpected seems a better outcome, sometimes it seems a worse outcome. As we saw in the exercise above, in our lives, as in our research, things do not always go according to plan. This is one of the reasons why we like to use the AID Self-Correcting method with Conversational Storytelling Interviews.

Whatever happens in the research process, use it for your benefit. A 'negative' result is just information. Remember how Eccles turned failure into a Nobel Prize. Grace Ann used 'restorying' to turn her situation of failing nine students for cheating into a 'teachable moment' where everyone could benefit (Rosile 2007). If we use the 'six Bs' of Antenarrative, we can prepare for the future we want, making it more likely to happen. Then if that fails, we can restory. We hope you find these methods helpful, enjoyable, and meaningful in your research and in your life.

CAUTION: the list below is a *JOKE*. It is not to be confused with any University's actual policies and procedures (although it may be hard to tell the difference sometimes)!

DR. ROSILE'S ULTIMATE PHD COMPLETION PROGRAM

(Copyright 2008, not to be cited without permission of author)

Most who have not completed a dissertation do not realize that after the defense, there is still quite a bit of detailed work to be done, to be sure your dissertation manuscript is in proper order with correct type of font, size of margins, style of footnotes, binding, etc. etc. etc., and then there is all the University paperwork to complete. These processes and procedures are NECESSARY for the awarding of the PhD, but they are NOT SUFFICIENT for the integration of the new role into the deeper personality structures of the freshly-minted PhD.

The Ultimate PhD Completion Program's 10 Prerequisite steps are the only tested, proven, and accredited process, which is both NECESSARY and SUFFICIENT, to prepare the PhD candidate for shedding the deeply-embedded role of STUDENT (poverty-stricken-works-for-slave-wages) and embracing a new role as productive (those articles never end) and respected (sometimes even by your students) working (by now you are already halfway to retirement) PROFESSIONAL (you'd never know it by the behavior of many of our colleagues).

10 Prerequisites for the Ultimate PhD Completion Program

1. You must celebrate completion with each family member/friend you encounter throughout one full year after your defense. Celebrate at least once with each person, and more than once is also allowed.
2. You must have some memorable tangible symbol for yourself, from yourself and/or loved ones. Diamonds work well. Like your PhD, they are forever.
3. You must frame your diploma. Even better is shrinking a color copy of your diploma and putting it in a 4x6 frame so it will fit in the miniscule offices normally given to junior faculty.
4. You must attend your graduation. Only such a large event, with lots of aggravating herding of people into places, and endless boring and occasionally inspirational speeches, will convince your mind that you are truly DONE.
5. Be sure someone you love is there with you at graduation.

6. Get someone you love not as much, to go to your graduation to hold the camera necessary for the multitude of photos needed for all those people who said to your parents 'S/he's STILL in school??? What is s/he doing??? And s/he's not going to be a REAL doctor???'

7. If you are going to be in academia, consider spending a bit on a decent cap and gown as you could be wearing them once or twice a year from now until retirement. And for women, some prefer the beret-style cap to the mortarboard. The regalia can also come in handy at Halloween.

8. CAUTION: Post-traumatic stress syndrome is common among graduates, most often in the form of flashbacks. The arduous process of coursework and dissertation has been with you for so long, it will take at least the full year of celebrating (prerequisite #1) and seeing your tangible symbol (prerequisite #2) before you will stop having flashbacks and suddenly think to yourself 'oh, I forgot, I'm DONE!'

9. MOST IMPORTANT: Completing the PhD is its own reward! If none of the above steps are completed, you will still be walking about 12' above the ground! You will feel so good about yourself, that all the gifts, accolades, and parties will feel trivial in comparison – but be gracious anyway.

10. FINALLY: The only ones who will be happier and prouder than you at your completion are your LOVED ONES who vicariously lived through the traumas and tribulations all these years. Indulge them by sharing your happiness, and remember that Prerequisite #1 is for them as much as for you!

CONGRATULATIONS!!

References

Allen, R., J. Packer, J. C. Eccles, H. N. Parton, H. G. Forder, and K. R. Popper (1945). Research and the University: A Statement by a Group of Teachers in the University of New Zealand. A two-page pamphlet. Christchurch, NZ.

Arendt, Hannah (1978). *The Life of the Mind: Willing.* Vol. 2. London, New York: Harcourt Brace Javanovich.

Aristotle (written 350 BCE/1954). *Aristotle: Rhetoric and Poetics.* Intro by Friedrich Solmsen; Rhetoric translated by W. Rhys Roberts; Poetics translated by Ingram Bywater. NY: The Modern Library (Random House). Citing the Rhetoric book on-line, accessed 11 March 2019 at http://www.bocc.ubi.pt/pag/Aristotle-rhetoric .pdf and Poetics at https://www.gutenberg.org/files/1974/1974-h/1974-h.htm.

Bakhtin, M. M. (1981). *The Dialogic Imagination: Four Essays.* Edited by Michael Holquist; Translated by Caryl Emerson and Michael Holquist. Austin, TX: University of Texas Press.

Bakhtin, M. M. (1990). *Art and Answerability: Early Philosophical Essays* (Vol. 9). Foreword by Michael Holquist; Translated with Vadim Liapunov. Austin, TX: University of Texas Press.

Bakhtin, M. M. (1993). *Toward a Philosophy of the Act.* Written as unpublished notebooks between 1919–1921, first published in the USSR in 1986 with the title *K filosofii postupka*; 1993 English Translation, V. Liapunov, V. Liapunov, and M. Holquist (eds). Austin, TX: University of Texas Press.

Bamberg, M. and M. Andrews (eds) (2004). *Considering Counter-Narratives. Narrating, Resisting, Making Sense.* Amsterdam and Philadelphia: John Benjamins.

Barad, K. (2003). Posthumanist performativity: toward an understanding of how matter comes to matter. *Signs: Journal of Women in Culture and Society*, 28(3): 801–31. Available on-line at http://www.kiraoreilly.com/blog/wp-content/uploads/2009/06/ signsbarad.pdf.

Barad, K. (2007). *Meeting the Universe Halfway: Quantum Physics and the Entanglement of Matter and Meaning.* Durham, NC, London: Duke University Press.

Barad, K. (2008). Queer causation and the ethics of mattering. In Noreen Giffney and Myra J. Hird (eds), *Queering the Non/Human.* Hampshire, England/Burlington, VT: Ashgate Publishing, 311–38.

Benjamin, Walter (1928/2016). *One-way Street.* Original 1928, 2016 edition with Preface. Translated by Edmund Jephcott, edited with intro by Michael W. Jennings, and preface by Greil Marcus. Cambridge, MA, London: The Belknap Press of Harvard University Press.

Bennett, J. (2008). *Vibrant Matter: A Political Ecology of Things.* Durham, NC: Duke University Press.

Bennett, Jane (2010). A vitalist stopover on the way to a new materialism. In Diana Coole and Samantha Frost (eds), *New Materialisms: Ontology, Agency, and Politics.* Durham, NC: Duke University Press, 47–69.

Berger, P. L., and T. Luckmann (1967). *The Social Construction of Reality: Everything that Passes for Knowledge in Society.* London: Allen Lane.

Bergson, Henri (1960). *Time and Free-Will: An Essay on the Immediate Data of Consciousness.* Translation by F. L. Pogson. New York: Harper and Row.

Bergson, Henri (1988). *Matter and Memory.* Translation by Nancy Margaret Paul and W. Scott Palmer. New York: Zone Books.

Bloc, Vincent (2019). Nothing else matters: Towards an ontological concept of the materiality of the earth in the age of global warming. *Research in Phenomenology*, 49: 65–87. Accessed 11 March 2019 at https://www.academia.edu/keypass/SnZwL1F6TjFzaVN2akNDT1lxQ2dDMEVkVE51bjBSNFQrZlA5Ym lacnF2TT0tLXkxd2VpM2c1R3A2bWswVk9OaVFHQXc9PQ==--871e 9faae2dc8c65e099bff573292b5c7d20ce5e/t/KAxn-MYnLVd4-bmWBki/attachments/58580093/download_file.

Block, W. E., and P. L. Nelson (2015). *Water Capitalism: The Case for Privatizing Oceans, Rivers, Lakes, and Aquifers.* Lanham, MD: Lexington Books.

Boje, D. M. (1991). The storytelling organization: A study of story performance in an office-supply firm. *Administrative Science Quarterly*, 36(1): 106–26.

Boje, D. M. (1995). Stories of the storytelling organization: A postmodern analysis of Disney as 'Tamara-Land'. *Academy of Management Journal*, 38(4): 997–1035.

Boje, D. M. (2001). *Narrative Methods for Organizational and Communication Research.* Thousand Oaks, CA: Sage.

Boje, D. M. (2008). *Storytelling Organizations.* Thousand Oaks, CA: Sage.

Boje, D. M. (2010a). Side shadowing appreciative inquiry: One storyteller's commentary. *Journal of Management Inquiry*, 19(3): 238–41.

Boje, D. M. (2010b). Narrative analysis. In A. J. Mills, G. Durepos, and E. Wiebe (eds), *Sage Encyclopedia of Case Study Research* (Vol. II). Thousand Oaks, CA: Sage, 591–4,

Boje, D. M. (2011a). Introduction to agential antenarratives that shape the future of organizations. In D. Boje (ed.), *Storytelling and the Future of Organizations.* London: Routledge, 19–38.

Boje, D. M. (2011b). Preface to qualimetrics. In H. Savall and V. Zardet (eds), *The Qualimetrics Approach: Observing the Complex Object.* Charlotte, NC: Information Age Publishing (IAP), xii–xx.

Boje, D. M. (2012). Reflections: What does quantum physics of storytelling mean for change management? *Journal of Change Management*, 12(3): 253–271. Accessed 11 March 2019 at https://davidboje.com/vita/paper_pdfs/JCM_BojeReflections _July 21 2011.pdf.

Boje, D. M. (2014). *Storytelling Organizational Practices: Managing in the Quantum Age.* London: Routledge.

Boje, D. M. (2016a). *Organizational Change and Global Standardization: Solutions to the Standards and Norms Overwhelming Organizations.* London, New York: Routledge.

Boje, D. M. (2016b). SEAM's 'Storytelling Dialectical Method' and the Failure of Appreciative Inquiry as a Scientific Method of Organizational Development and Change. Conference presentation to The 'Organization Development and Change' Division and the 'Management Consulting' Division of the Academy of Management (USA), 9–10 June 2016, Lyon, France.

Boje, D. M. (2016c). But that's not a story! Antenarrative dialectics between and beneath indigenous living story and western narratives. In Grace Ann Rosile (ed.),

Tribal Wisdom for Business Ethics. Bingley, UK: Emerald Group Publishing Limited, 69–72.

Boje, D. M. (2016d). Critique of the triple bottom line. In Grace Ann Rosile (ed.), *Tribal Wisdom for Business Ethics*. Bingley, UK: Emerald Group Publishing Limited, 181–98.

Boje, D. M. (2017a). *Theaters of Capitalism: Creating Conscious Capitalism*. Las Cruces, NM: TamaraLand Publishing.

Boje, D. M. (2017b). How does Quantum Storytelling Relate to Savall's Socioeconomic Double Spiral? Proceedings Paper, written 17 November 2017 for the 7th annual Quantum Storytelling Conference, 14–16 December 2017. Accessed 5 May 2020 at   http://davidboje.com/quantum/pdfs_quantum_2017/Boje_SEAM_DOUBLE _SPIRALS_and_STORYTELLING.htm.

Boje, D. M. (2018a). Preface: 'Global capitalism is unsustainable' for H. Savall, Michel Peron, V. Zardet, and Marc Bonnet, *Socially Responsible Capitalism*. London: Routledge.

Boje, D. M. (2018b). The Interplay of Philosophy of Science, Statistics, and Storytelling. Accepted 20 January 2018. To appear in Adebowale Akande, Bolanle Adetoun, and Modupe Adewuyi (eds), *Nova International Handbook of Psychology*. see on-line prepublication pdf.

Boje, D. (2018c). Risky double spiral sensemaking of Academic Capitalism. In R. P. Gephart, C. C. Miller, and K. S. Helgesson (eds), *Routledge Companion to Risk, Crisis and Emergency Management*. London: Routledge, Chapter 22.

Boje, D. M. (2018d). Seven True Storytelling Solutions to the Global Water Crisis. Proceeding paper for 8th Annual Quantum Storytelling Conference, 13 December 2018. Accessed 9 February 2019 at http://davidboje.com/388/2018%20storytelling %20conference%20BOJE%20_%20True%20Storytelling%20of%20New %20Mexico%20Water.docx.

Boje, D. M. (2019a). *Global Storytelling: There is No Planet B*. Singapore, London, New York: World Scientific.

Boje, D. M. (2019b). *Organizational Research: Storytelling in Action*. London, New York: Routledge.

Boje, D. M. (2019c, *in press*). *Storytelling Interventions in Global Water Crisis*. Singapore, London, New York: World Scientific.

Boje, D. M., and Yue Cai-Hillon (2017). The fifth epoch: socio-economic approach to sustainable capitalism markets, *Globalization and Development Review*, 2(2). Accessed 5 May 2020 at http://digitalcommons.uri.edu/cgi/viewcontent.cgi?article =1029&context=mgdr.

Boje, D. M., and Robert F. Dennehy (1993). *Managing in the Postmodern World: America's Revolution against Exploitation*. Dubuque, IA: IAP.

Boje, D. M., and T. L. Henderson (eds) (2014). *Being Quantum: Ontological Storytelling in the Age of Antenarrative*. UK: Cambridge Scholars Publishing.

Boje, D., and G. A. Rosile (2003a). Theatrics of SEAM. *Journal of Organizational Change Management*, 16(1): 21–32.

Boje, D., and G. A. Rosile (2003b). Comparison of socio-economic and other transorganizational development methods. *Journal of Organizational Change Management*, 16(1): 10–20.

Boje, D. M., and G. A. Rosile (2008). Specters of Wal-Mart: A critical discourse analysis of stories of Sam Walton's ghost. *Critical Discourse Studies*, 5(2): 153–79.

Boje, D. M. and G. A. Rosile (2015). Equine-assisted Restorying for Veterans and Their Loved Ones. Presentation at the annual conference of the Equine Assisted Growth and Learning Association (EAGALA), Utah, March 2015.

Boje, D. M., and Mabel Sanchez (eds) (2019a). *The Emerald Handbook of Quantum Storytelling Consulting*. Bingley, UK: Emerald Press

Boje, D. M., and Mabel Sanchez (eds) (2019b). *The Emerald Handbook of Management and Organizational Inquiry*. Bingley, UK: Emerald Press.

Boje, D. M., and Rohny Saylors (2013). Q 4 Virtuality and materiality in the ethics of storytelling. In Rune Todnem By and Bernard Burnes (eds), *Organizational Change, Leadership and Ethics: Leading Organizations towards Sustainability*. London: Routledge, 75–96.

Boje, D. M., and Hank Strevel (2016). Feature choice: Using Quantum Storytelling to bridge appreciative inquiry to socio-economic approach to intervention research. *AI Practitioner: International Journal of Appreciative Inquiry*, 18(3): 79–89.

Boje, D. M., Carolyn L. Gardner, and William L. Smith (2006). (Mis)Using numbers in the Enron Story. *Organizational Research Methodologies Journal*, 9(4): 456–74.

Boje, D. M., R. P. Gephart, and T. J. Thatchenkery (1996). *Postmodern Management and Organization Theory*. Thousand Oaks, CA; Sage.

Boje, D. M., E. Gergerich, and M. Svane (2016). Fractal change management and counter-narrative in cross-cultural change. In S. Frandsen, T. Kuhn, and M. Wolff Lundholt (eds), *Counter-narratives and Organization*, London: Routledge, 137–62.

Boje, D. M., U. C. Haley, and R. Saylors (2016). Antenarratives of organizational change: The microstoria of Burger King's storytelling in space, time and strategic context. *Human Relations*, 69(2): 391–418.

Boje, D. M., Jens Larsen, and Lena Bruun (2017). True Storytelling: How to Succeed with Your Implementation. Working paper. Accessed 5 May 2020 at http://oldfriendsindustries.com/?page_id=1048.

Boje, D. M., C. Oswick, and J. D. Ford (2004). Language and organization: The doing of discourse. *Academy of Management Review*, 29(4): 571–7.

Boje, D. M., M. Svane, and E. Gergerich (2016). Counternarrative and antenarrative inquiry in two cross-cultural contexts. *European Journal of Cross-Cultural Competence and Management*, 4(1): 55–84.

Boje, D. M., H. Baca-Greif, M. Intindola, and S. Elias (2017). The episodic spiral model: A new approach to organizational processes. *Journal of Organizational Change Management*, 30(5): 683–709.

Boundas, Constantin V. (2010). Virtual/Virtuality. In Adrian Parr (ed.), *The Deleuze Dictionary Revised Edition*. Edinburgh: Edinburgh University Press, 300–2.

Broadbent, J. (2002). Critical accounting research: A view from England. *Critical Perspectives on Accounting*, 13(4): 433–49.

Burke, K. (1945). *A Grammar of Motives.* Berkeley, CA: University of California Press.

Butler J. (2004). *Undoing Gender*. London: Routledge.

Butler J. (2005). *Giving an Account of Oneself.* New York: Fordham University Press.

Cai-Hillon, Y., G. Kisiel, and M. E. Hillon (2016). A discursive framework for research in management consulting. *Recherches en Sciences de Gestion* (6): 109–24.

Cajete, G. (1993). An enchanted land: spiritual ecology and a theology of place. *Winds of Change*, 8(2): 50–3.

Cajete, Gregory (1994). *Look to the Mountain: An Ecology of Indigenous Education*. Durango, CO: Kivaki Press.

Cajete, G. (1999). *A People's Ecology: Explorations in Sustainable Living*. Santa Fe, NM: Clear Light Publishers.

Cajete, G. (2000). *Native Science: Natural Laws of Interdependence*. Santa Fe, NM: Clear Light Publishers.

Cajete, G. (2015). *Indigenous Community: Rekindling the Teachings of the Seventh Fire*. Foreword by James Sa'ke'j Youngblood Henderson. St. Paul, MN: Living Justice Press.

Cameron, K., and J. Dutton (eds) (2003). *Positive Organizational Scholarship: Foundations of a New Discipline*. San-Francisco, CA: Berrett-Koehler Publishers.

Charmaz, K. (2006). *Constructing Grounded Theory: A Practical Guide through Qualitative Analysis*. London: Sage.

Chiapello, E. (2017). Critical accounting research and neoliberalism. *Critical Perspectives on Accounting*, 43: 47–64.

Clark, J. (2005). Teaching and research: The Canterbury Declaration and Popper's legacy for teacher educators. *New Zealand Annual Review of Education*, 14(2004): 111–30.

Clark, P., and M. Rowlinson (2002). Time and narrative history in organization theory: Charting historical narratives. In *Academy of Management Meeting, Organization and Management Theory Division*, Denver, August.

Compton, W. C., and E. Hoffman (2019). *Positive Psychology: The Science of Happiness and Flourishing*. London: SAGE Publications.

Cooper, D. J., and D. Neu (1995). The politics of debt and deficit in Alberta. In G. Laxer and T. Harrison (eds), *The Trojan Horse: Alberta and the Future of Canada*, Black Rose Books, 163–81.

Cooperrider, D. (2001). Appreciative Inquiry: The Positive Core of Change. Paper presented at the meeting of the Minnesota OD Network, University of St. Thomas, MN., October 2001.

Cooperrider, David L., and Diana Whitney (2019). A Positive Revolution in Change: Appreciative Inquiry. Draft accessed 11 March 2019 at https://www.academia.edu/38504721/A_Positive_Revolution_in_Change_Appreciative_Inqui?email_work_card=view-paper.

Corbin, J., and A. Strauss (2007). *Basics of Developing Grounded Theory*. London: Sage.

Czarniawska, B. (ed.) (1998). *A Narrative Approach to Organization Studies* (Qualitative Research Methods Series, Vol. 43). Thousand Oaks, CA: Sage Publications.

Czarniawska, B. (2004). *Narratives in Social Science Research*. London: Sage.

Deleuze. Gilles (1990). *Logic of Sense*. New York: Columbia University Press.

Deleuze, Gilles (1991). *Bergsonism*. Translated by Hugh Tomlinson and Barbara Habberjam. New York: Zone Books.

Deleuze, Gilles (1994). *Difference and Repetition*. Translated by Paul Patton. New York: Columbia University Press.

Deleuze, Gilles (1997). *Essays Critical and Clinical*. Translated by D. W. Smith and M. A. Greco. Minneapolis, MN: University of Minnesota Press.

Deleuze, Gilles, and Felix Guattari (1987). *A Thousand Plateaus: Capitalism and Schizophrenia*. Translation and Foreword by Brian Massumi. Minneapolis, MN: University of Minnesota Press. Accessed 25 March 2019 at https://www.ntnu.no/wiki/download/attachments/21463142/deleuzeguattarirhizome.pdf.

Deleuze, Gilles, and Felix Guattari (1994). *What is Philosophy*. Translated by Hugh Tomlinson and Graham Burchell. New York: Columbia University Press.

Drass, Kriss A., and Charles C. Ragin (1992). *Qualitative Comparative Analysis 3.0*. Evanston, IL: Institute for Policy Research, Northwestern University.

Eccles, J. C. (1945). Principles of Scientific Method: Notes on Five Lectures by Dr. K. R. Popper, given at the University of Otago from 22 to 26 May 1945. Accessed 8 March 2019 at http://popper-prior.nz/items/show/208.

Eccles, J. C. (1970/2013). *Facing Reality: Philosophical Adventures by a Brain Scientist*. First published Berlin/Heidelberg, Germany: Springer Science and Business Media.

Flora, K. (2019). Second wave of positive psychology: beyond the dichotomy of positive and negative and the consequences in the practice of psychotherapy. *Counselling Psychology Quarterly*, 32(3-4): 333–40.

Flora, J., D. Boje, G. A. Rosile, and K. Hacker (2016). A theoretical and applied review of embodied restorying for post-deployment family reintegration. *Journal of Veterans Studies*, 1(1): 129–62.

Foucault, M. (1984). *The Foucault Reader*. New York: Pantheon.

Franzosi, R. (ed.) (2010). *Quantitative Narrative Analysis* (No. 162). London: Sage.

Freire, P. (1970/2000). *Pedagogy of the Oppressed*. 2000 is the 50th anniversary edition. Translated by Myra Bergman Ramos with Foreword by Shaull, and an Introduction by Donaldo Macedo. New York: The Continuum International Publishing Group Inc. Accessed 26 March 2019 at http://web.msu.ac.zw/elearning/material/1335344125freire_pedagogy_of_the_oppresed.pdf.

Gabriel, Y. (2000). *Storytelling in Organisations*, Oxford: Oxford University Press.

Gabriel, Y. (2016). Narrative ecologies and the role of counter-narratives: The case of nostalgic stories and conspiracy theories. In S. Frandsen, T. Kuhn, and M. W. Lundholt (eds), *Counter-Narrative and Organizations*. London: Routledge.

Gephart, R. P. (1988). *Ethnostatistics: Qualitative Foundations for Quantitative Research*. Thousand Oaks, CA: SAGE Publications, Inc.

Gladstone, J. S. (2015). Native American Transplanar Wisdom. In C. Spiller and R. Wolfgramm (eds), *Indigenous Spiritualities at Work: Transforming the Spirit of Enterprise*. Charlotte, NC: Information Age Press, 21–32.

Glaser, B. G. (1992). *Basics of Grounded Theory: Emergence vs. Forcing*. Mill Valley, CA: Sociology Press.

Glaser, B. G. (2001). *The Grounded Theory Perspective: Conceptualization Contrasted with Description*. Mill Valley, CA: Sociology Press.

Glaser, B. G. (2002). Constructivist grounded theory?, *Forum: Qualitative sozialforschung* 3(3). Accessed 5 May 2020 at http://www.qualitative-research.net/fqs-texte/3-02/3-02glaser-e.htm.

Glaser, B. G. (2003). *The Grounded Theory Perspective II: Description's Remodeling of Grounded Theory Methodology*, Mill Valley, CA, Sociology Press

Glaser, B. G. (2004). Naturalist inquiry and grounded theory, *Forum: Qualitative Sozialforschung*, 5(1). Accessed 5 May 2020 at http://www.qualitative-research.net/fqs-texte/1-04/1-04glaser-e.htm.

Glaser, B. G. (2005). *The Grounded Theory Perspective III: Theoretical Coding*. Mill Valley, CA, Sociology Press.

Glaser, B. G. (2007). Doing formal theory. In *The Sage Handbook of Grounded Theory* (Part II). Thousand Oaks, CA: Sage, 97–113.

Glaser, B. G. (2008). *Doing Quantitative Grounded Theory*. Mill Valley, CA: Sociology Press.

Glaser, B. G., and J. Holton (2004). Remodeling grounded theory. *Forum: Qualitative sozialforschung*, 5(2). Accessed 5 May 2020 at http://www.qualitative-research.net/index.php/fqs/article/view/607/1315.

Glaser, B., and G. A. L. Strauss (1967). *The Discovery of Grounded Theory: Strategies for Qualitative Research*. London: Wiedenfeld and Nicholson.

Gray, R., A. Brennan, and J. Malpas (2014). New accounts: Towards a reframing of social accounting. *Accounting Forum*, 38(4): 258–73.

Gray, R., J. Malpas, and A. Brennan (2014). New accounts of old accounts, the chatter of silence and not being who we are not. *Accounting Forum*, 38(4): 296–8.

Friedman, M. (1991). The re-evaluation of logical positivism. *Journal of Philosophy*, 88(10): 505–19. Accessed 13 March 2019 at https://www.jstor.org/stable/pdf/2027094.pdf.

Hacohen, M. H. (2000). *Karl Popper – The Formative Years, 1902–1945*. Cambridge, UK: Cambridge University Press.

Haley, U. C., and D. M. Boje (2014). Storytelling the internationalization of the multinational enterprise. *Journal of International Business Studies*, 45(9): 1115–32.

Haraway, D. J. (2016). *Staying with the Trouble: Making Kin in the Chthulucene*. Durham, NC: Duke University Press.

Hegel, G. W. F. (1807/1977). *Phenomenology of Spirit*. London, New York: Oxford University Press. Translated by A. V. Miller with analysis and Foreword, 1977, by J. N. Findlay. We also cite the on-line version https://libcom.org/files/Phenomenology of Spirit – G. W. F. Hegel.mobi.

Hegel, G. W. F. (2010). *Georg Wilhelm Friedrich Hegel: The Science of Logic*. Cambridge: Cambridge University Press.

Heidegger, M. (1923/1988/1999). *Ontology – The Hermeneutics of Facticity*. Translated by John van Buren. Lecture given 1923/German publication 1988/English publication 1999. Bloomington and Indianapolis, IN: Indiana University Press.

Heidegger, M. (1927/1962). *Being and Time*. Translated 1962 by John Macquarrie and Edward Robinson. New York: Harper Row.

Heidegger, M. (2003). *Four Seminars: Le Thor 1966, 1968, 1969, Zahringen 1973*. Translated by Andrew Mitchell and François Raffoul. Bloomington and Indianapolis. IN: Indiana University Press. First published in German 1977.

Henderson, T. L., and D. M. Boje, (2016). *Managing Fractal Organizing Processes*. New York and London: Routledge.

Hitchin, L. (2015). Method and story fragments. In M. Izak, L. Hitchin, and D. Anderson (eds), *Untold Stories in Organizations*. London: Routledge, 213–38.

Holton, J. A. (2008). Grounded theory as a general research methodology. *The Grounded Theory Review*, 7(2): 67–89. Accessed 23 March 2019 at https://formamente.guideassociation.org/wp-content/uploads/2009_1_2_holton.pdf.

Jacobs, K. (2011). Enlightenment and emancipation: Reflections for critical accounting research. *Critical Perspectives on Accounting*, 22(5): 510–15.

Jørgensen, K. M., and D. M. Boje (2020 forthcoming/*in press*). Storytelling sustainability in problem-based learning. In R. V. Turcan and J. R. Reilly (eds), *Populism in Higher Education Curriculum Development – Problem-based Learning as a Mitigating Response*. London: Palgrave Macmillan.

Kant, I. (1785/1993). *Grounding for the Metaphysics of Morals: On a Supposed Right to Lie because of Philanthropic Concerns*. Translated by James W. Ellington. German 1785, 3rd edition 1993. Indianapolis, IN: Hackett Publishing Company, Inc.

Kant, I. (1889). *Critique of Practical Reason and Other Works on the Theory of Ethics*. Translated by Thomas Kingsmill Abbott, 4th revised edition. London: Longmans,

Green and Co. Accessed 5 May 2020 at http://oll.libertyfund.org/title/360/61767/641368 on 2011-09-01.

Kelle, U. (2007). 'Emergence' vs. 'forcing' of empirical data? A crucial problem of 'grounded theory' reconsidered. *Historical Social Research, Supplement* (19): 133–56.

Kirkeby, O. F. (2000). *Management Philosophy: A Radical-Normative Perspective.* Berlin: Springer Science and Business Media.

Kirkeby, O. F. (2008). *The Virtue of Leadership.* Denmark: Copenhagen Business School Press.

Kirkeby, O. F. (2009). *The New Protreptic: The Concept and the Art.* Denmark: Copenhagen Business School Press.

Klepp, S., and J. Herbeck (2016). The politics of environmental migration and climate justice in the Pacific region. *Journal of Human Rights and the Environment*, 7(1): 54–73.

Kuhn, T. (1962). *The Structure of Scientific Revolutions.* Accessed 13 March 2019 at https://projektintegracija.pravo.hr/_download/repository/Kuhn_Structure_of_Scientific_Revolutions.pdf.

Larsen, J., L. Bruun, and D. M. Boje (*in press*). *True Storytelling.* London: Routledge.

Laughlin, R. (1999). Critical accounting: nature, progress and prognosis. *Accounting, Auditing and Accountability Journal*, 21(1): 73–8.

Loomis, E. (2013). The global water crisis: Privatization and neocolonialism in film. *Radical History Review*, (116): 189–95.

Love, T. R. (2017a). Māori Values, Care and Compassion in Organisations: A Research Strategy. In the proceedings of the European Group for Organizational Studies Symposium. Copenhagen Business School, Copenhagen, Denmark, 6–7 July 2017.

Love, T. R. (2017b). Mana, Māori (Indigenous New Zealand) and Critical Studies of Management in Aotearoa New Zealand. In the proceedings of the Critical Management Studies Conference. Britannia Adelphi Hotel, Liverpool, UK, 3–5 July 2017.

Love, T. R. (2018a). Organizing Indigenous-Māori Identities at Work. In the proceedings of the European Group for Organizational Studies Symposium. Tallinn, Estonia. 5–7 July 2018.

Love, T. R. (2018b). Anteresearch in Indigenous Organization Studies. In the proceedings of the Gender, Work and Organisation Conference, Macquarie University, Sydney, 13–16 June 2018.

Love, T. R. (2019a). *Indigenous Organization Studies: Exploring Management, Business and Community.* Cham, Switzerland: Palgrave Macmillan.

Love, T. R. (2019b). Indigenous knowledges, priorities and processes in qualitative organizations and management research: State of the field. *Qualitative Research in Organizations and Management*, 15(1): 6–20.

Love, T. R. (2020). Care and compassion at work: Theorizing indigenous knowledges in colonial contexts. In M. Fotaki, G. Islam, and A. Antoni (eds), *Business Ethics and Care in Organizations.* New York: Routledge.

Love, T. R., J. Finsterwalder, and A. Tombs (2017). Māori knowledge and consumer tribes. *MAI: A New Zealand Journal of Indigenous Research*, 7(1): 44–50.

Lyotard, Jean-François (1979/1984). *The Postmodern Condition: A Report on Knowledge* (Vol. 10). Translated from the 1979 Les Editions de Minuit in 1984 by Geoffrey Bennington and Brian Massumi. Minneapolis, MN: University of Minnesota Press. Accessed 8 March 2019 at https://monoskop.org/images/e/e0/

Lyotard_Jean-Francois_The_Postmodern_Condition_A_Report_on_Knowledge
.pdf.

Macfarlane, A. H. (2012). 'Other' education down-under: Indigenizing the discipline for psychologists and specialist educators. *Other Education: The Journal of Educational Alternatives*, 1(1): 205–25.

Neu, D., D. J. Cooper, and J. Everett (2001). Critical accounting interventions. *Critical Perspectives on Accounting*, 12(6): 735–62.

Nietzsche, F. W. (1968). *The Will to Power*. Translation by Walter Kaufmann and R. J. Hollingdale, edited with commentary by Walter Kaufmann. New York: Vintage books. Sometimes I cite the on-line version, accessed 27 February 2019 at https:// archive.org/stream/FriedrichNietzscheTheWillToPower/Friedrich%20Nietzsche %20-%20The%20Will%20to%20Power_djvu.txt.

Peirce, C. S. (1931–1935). *Collected Papers of Charles Sanders Peirce*. Volumes I–VI, edited by Charles Hartshorne and Paul Weiss, 1931–1935. Cambridge, MA: Harvard University Press.

Peirce, C. S. (1931/1960). *Collected Papers of Charles Sanders Peirce*. Vol I Principles of Philosophy and Vol II Elements of Logic. Edited by Charles Hartshorne and Paul Weiss. Cambridge, MA: The Belknap Press of Harvard University Press.

Peirce, C. S. (1933–1937). *Collected Papers of Charles Sanders Peirce*. Edited by Charles Hartshorne and Paul Weiss. Volumes 1 to 8. Cambridge, MA: Harvard University Press.

Peirce, C. S. (1958). *Collected Papers of Charles Sanders Peirce*. Volumes VII–VIII, edited by Arthur W. Burks, 1958. Cambridge, MA: Harvard University Press.

Penrose, R. (2011). Godel, the mind, and the laws of physics. In Matthias Baaz, Christos H. Papadimitriou, Hilary W. Putnam, Dana S. Scott, and Charles L. Harper Jr. (eds), *Kurt Gödel and the Foundations of Mathematics: Horizons of Truth*. Cambridge, New York: Cambridge University Press. 339–60.

Pihkala, S., and H. Karasti (2018). Politics of mattering in the practices of participatory design. In August Proceedings of the 15th Participatory Design Conference: Short Papers, Situated Actions, Workshops and Tutorial – Vol. 2 (p. 13), Hasselt and Genk, Belgium, 20–24 August 2018.

Plato (428–348 BCE). *The Dialogues of Plato*. Translated by Benjamin Jowett. Etext edition by Antonio Gonzalez Fernandez. Accessed 12 January 2018 at http://webs .ucm.es/info/diciex/gente/agf/plato/The_Dialogues_of_Plato_v0.1.pdf.

Polkinghorne, D. E. (1988). *Narrative Knowing and the Human Sciences*. Albany, NY: State of New York University Press.

Polkinghorne, D. E. (2004). Narrative therapy and postmodernism. In Lynne, E. Angus, and John McLeod (eds), *The Handbook of Narrative and Psychotherapy: Practice, Theory and Research*. Thousand Oaks, CA: Sage Publications, 53–68.

Popper, K. R. (1935/1959/1992/2000). *The Logic of Scientific Discovery*. Logik der Forschung first published 1935 by Verlag von Julius Springer, Vienna, Austria. First English translation by Hutchinson and Co., then 1992 by London: Routledge, and again by Routledge Classics 2000. Accessed 6 March 2019 at http://strangebeautiful .com/other-texts/popper-logic-scientific-discovery.pdf and from http://www.math .chalmers.se/~ulfp/Review/logicscdis.pdf.

Popper, K. R. (1945/2008). *After the Open Society: Selected Social and Political Writings*. First published 1945, then in 2008 edited by Jeremy Shearmur and Piers Norris Turner. London, New York: Routledge.

Popper, K. R. (1945/2012). *The Open Society and its Enemies*. First published 1945 by Routledge and Kegan Paul. 2012 edition by London: Routledge.

Popper, K. R. (1956/1982). *Quantum Theory and the Schism in Physics.* From the *Postscript to the Logic of Scientific Discovery*, edited by W. W. Bartley, III. Author's note and preface are 1982, rest is 1956. London, Sydney, Auckland: Hutchinson and Co. (Publishers) Ltd.

Popper, K. R. (1956/1983). *Realism and the Aim of Science.* From the *Postscript to the Logic of Scientific Discovery*, edited by W. W. Bartley, III. Includes a 1956 Preface, and Introduction, 1982, and published together 1983. London, UK: Hutchinson and Co. (Publishers) Ltd.

Popper, K. R. (1963). *Conjectures and Refutations: The Growth of Scientific Knowledge.* London: Routledge and Kegan Paul.

Popper, K. R. (1972). *Objective Knowledge* (Vol. 360). Oxford: Oxford University Press. Accessed 7 March 2019 at https://pdfs.semanticscholar.org/845d/20c52e47cfb37 9ba1e384de92ed78eaac3ad.pdf.

Popper, K. (1973). *Objective Knowledge: An Evolutionary Approach* (2nd corrected edition). Oxford: Oxford University Press.

Popper, K. R. (1978). The Three Worlds. The Tanner Lecture on Human Values. Delivered at The University of Michigan, 7 April 1978. Accessed 10 March 2019 at https://tannerlectures.utah.edu/_documents/a-to-z/p/popper80.pdf, 141–67.

Popper, K. R. (1979/2014). Die beiden Grundprobleme der Erkenntnistheorie, Hrsg. *Troels Eggers Hansen. Tübingen: JCB Mohr (Paul Siebeck).* The book was translated to English as K. Popper, (2014). *The Two Fundamental Problems of the Theory of Knowledge.* Translated by Andreas Pickel and edited by Troels Eggers Hansen. London: Routledge. Accessed 6 March 2019 at https://content.taylorfrancis .com/books/download?dac=C2010-0-41626-X&isbn=9781135626761&format= googlePreviewPdf.

Popper, K. R. (1994). *The Myth of the Framework: In Defense of Science and Rationality.* Edited by M.S. Notturno. London, New York: Routledge.

Popper, K. R. (2008). *After the Open Society: Selected Social and Political Writings of Karl Popper.* Edited by Jeremy Shearmur and Piers Norris Turner. Abingdon: Routledge.

Pot, W. D., A. Dewulf, G. R. Biesbroek, and S. Verweij (2019). What makes decisions about urban water infrastructure forward looking? A fuzzy-set qualitative comparative analysis of investment decisions in 40 Dutch municipalities. *Land Use Policy*, 82: 781–95.

Price, D., and J. de Solla (1963). Little science, big science ... and beyond. New York: Columbia University. Accessed 24 March 2019 at http://www.andreasaltelli.eu/file/ repository/Little_science_big_science_and_beyond.pdf.

Ragin, C. C., Kriss A. Drass, and Sean Davey (2006). *Fuzzy-Set/Qualitative Comparative Analysis 2.0.* Tucson, AZ: Department of Sociology, University of Arizona.

Rahaman, A. S. (2010). Critical accounting research in Africa: Whence and whither. *Critical Perspectives on Accounting*, 21(5): 420–7.

Riach, K., N. Rumens, and M. Tyler (2016). Towards a Butlerian methodology: Undoing organizational performativity through anti-narrative research. *Human Relations*, 69(11): 2069–89. Accessed 28 August 2019 at https://journals.sagepub .com/doi/pdf/10.1177/0018726716632050.

Roberts, P. (2013). Academic dystopia: Knowledge, performativity, and tertiary education. *Review of Education, Pedagogy, and Cultural Studies*, 35(1): 27–43.

Roethlisberger, F. J., W. J. Dickson, H. A. Wright, and C. H. Pforzheimer (1939). Western Electric Company. Management and the Worker: An Account of a Research Program Conducted by the Western Electric Company, Hawthorne Works.

Roffe, J. (2010). Multiplicity. In Adrian Parr (ed.), *The Deleuze Dictionary Edition* (1st edition 2005). Edinburgh: Edinburgh University Press, 181–2.

Rosile, G. A. (2007). Cheating: Making it a teachable moment. *Journal of Management Education*, 31(5): 582–613.

Rosile, G. A. (2016). *Tribal Wisdom for Business Ethics*. Bingley, UK: Emerald Group Publishing Limited.

Rosile, G. A. and D. M. Boje (2002). Restorying and postmodern organization theatre: Consultation in the storytelling organization. In Ronald R. Sims (ed.), *Changing the Way We Manage Change*. Westport, CT, London: Quorum Books, 271–90.

Rosile, G. A., D. M Boje, and C. M. Claw (2018). Ensemble leadership theory: Collectivist, relational, and heterarchical roots from indigenous contexts. *Leadership*, 14(3): 307–28.

Rosile, G. A., D. M. Boje, D. M. Carlon, A. Downs, and R. Saylors (2013). Storytelling diamond: An antenarrative integration of the six facets of storytelling in organization research design. *Organizational Research Methods*, 16(4): 557–80.

Rosile, G. A., D. M. Boje, R. Herder, and M. Sanchez (2020 forthcoming). The coalition of Immokalee workers uses ensemble patchwork social movement to overcome enslavement in corporate supply chains. *Business and Society: Special Issue on Modern Day Slavery*.

Sartre, Jean Paul (1960/2004). *Critique of Dialectical Reason*, Vol. 1: Theory of practical ensembles. 1960 French *Critique de la Raison Dialectique*, Paris: Gallimard. 2004 English translation by Alan Sheridan-Smith, Foreword by Fredric Jameson. London, New York: Verso.

Savall, Henri (1975/2010). *Work and People: An Economic Evaluation of Job-Enrichment*. Translated by M. A. Woodhall. Charlotte, NC: Information Age Press.

Savall, H., and V. Zardet (2008). *Mastering Hidden Costs and Socio-Economic Performance*. Charlotte, NC: Information Age Press.

Savall, H., and V. Zardet (eds) (2011). *The Qualimetrics Approach: Observing the Complex Object*. Charlotte, NC: Information Age Press.

Savall, Henri, V. Zardet, and Marc Bonnet (2008). *Releasing the Untapped Potential of Enterprises through Socio-Economic Management*. 2nd Revised edition, 2008. London: International Labor Organization and Socio Economic Institute of Firms and Organizations.

Savall, H., Michel Peron, V. Zardet, and Marc. Bonnet (2018). *Socially Responsible Capitalism*. London: Routledge.

Saylors, R. and D. M. Boje, (*in review*). Contributions of Social Entrepreneurship To Narrative: Reconstructing United Nations' Goal 14 Life Below Water. *Strategic: Briefings in Entrepreneurial Finance* (journal).

Schopenhauer, Arthur. (1928). *The Philosophy of Schopenhauer*. Edited with Introduction by Irwin Edman. New York: The Modern Library.

Seidel, S., and C. Urquhart (2013). On emergence and forcing in information systems grounded theory studies: The case of Strauss and Corbin. *Journal of Information Technology*, 28(3): 237–60.

Sibel, James R. (2019). Beyond Culture: Social Exclusion Dynamics in the Lived Experience of Long-Term Undocumented Mexican Residents of the United States. PhD Diss., Cabrini University.

Skarmeas, D., C. N. Leonidou, and C. Saridakis (2014). Examining the role of CSR skepticism using fuzzy-set qualitative comparative analysis. *Journal of Business Research*, 67(9): 1796–805.

Smith, W. L., and D. M. Boje (2011). The rhetoric of toxic assets: An antenarrative analysis. In D. Boje (ed.), *Storytelling and the Future of Organizations*. London: Routledge, 334–46.

Smith, W. I., C. Gardner, and D. M. Boje (2004). Using the Ethnostatistics Methodology to reconcile rhetoric and reality: An examination of the management release of Enron's year end 2000 results. *Qualitative Research in Accounting and Management*, 1(2): 1–16.

Strand, Anete Mikkala Camille (2012). Enacting the Between: On Dis/continuous Intra-active Becoming of/through an Apparatus of Material Storytelling. Unpublished Doctoral Dissertation, Aalborg University, Denmark.

Strauss Anselm C., and Juliet Corbin (1990). *Basics of Qualitative Research: Grounded Theory Procedures and Techniques*, Newbury Park, CA: Sage Publications.

Strauss Anselm C., and Juliet Corbin (1994/1998). *Basics of Qualitative Research: Techniques and Procedures for Developing Grounded Theory*. 1st edition 1994. Thousand Oaks, CA: Sage Publications.

Stubbs, W., C. Higgins, and M. Milne (2013). Why do companies not produce sustainability reports? *Business Strategy and the Environment*, 22(7): 456–70.

Suddaby, Roy (2006). What grounded theory is not. *Academy of Management Journal* 49(4): 633–42.

Svane, M. (2018). Organizational-world creating: Being-in-becoming. A quantum relational process philosophy. In D. Boje and M. Sanchez (eds), *The Emerald Handbook of Quantum Storytelling Consulting*. Bingley, UK: Emerald Publishing, 245.

Svane, Marita S. (2019). Organizational storytelling of the future: Ante- and anti-narrative in quantum age. In D. Boje and M. Sanchez (eds), *The Emerald Handbook of Management and Organizational Inquiry*. Bingley, UK: Emerald Publishing, 153–82.

Svane, Marita, E. M. Gergerich, and David M. Boje (2017). Fractal change management and counter-narrative in cross-cultural change. In Sanne Frandsen, Timothy Kuhn, and Marianne Wolff Lundholt (eds), *Counter-Narratives and Organization*. New York: Routledge, 129–54.

Trafimow, David (2003). Hypothesis testing and theory evaluation at the boundaries: Surprising insights from Bayes's theorem. *Psychological Review*, 110(3): 526.

Trafimow, David. (2009). The theory of reasoned action: A case study of falsification in psychology. *Theory and Psychology*, 19(4), 501–18.

Trafimow, David (2012). The role of auxiliary assumptions for the validity of manipulations and measures. *Theory and Psychology*, 22: 486–98.

Trafimow, David (2014). Considering quantitative and qualitative issues together. *Qualitative Research in Psychology*, 11(1): 15–24.

Trafimow, David (2017). Implications of an initial empirical victory for the truth of the theory and additional empirical victories. *Philosophical Psychology*, 30(4): 415–37.

Trafimow, David (2018). Confidence intervals, precision and confounding. *New Ideas in Psychology*, 50: 48–53.

Trafimow, D. (2019). Five nonobvious changes in editorial practice for editors and reviewers to consider when evaluating submissions in a post p< 0.05 universe. *The American Statistician*, 73 (supl): 340–5.

Trafimow, D., and J. Uhalt (2015). The alleged tradeoff between explanatory breadth and predictive power. *Theory and Psychology*, 25(6): 833–40.

Trafimow, David, and J. Uhalt (*in press*). The quality of auxiliary assumptions depends upon connections to nonobservational terms in theories and observational terms in empirical hypotheses. *Theory and Psychology*.

TwoTrees, Kaylynn Sullivan (1997). Presentation at the Organizational Behavior Teaching conference, meeting at Case Western Reserve, Ohio, June 1997.

TwoTrees, Kaylynn Sullivan (2000). Seven directions practice: A practice for the crossroads, *The Fourth R* (92) August, September, October, published by CRENet.

TwoTrees, Kaylynn Sullivan, and Matthew Kolan (2016). The tress are breathing us: An indigenous view of relationship in nature and business. In Grace Ann Rosile (ed.), *Tribal Wisdom for Business Ethics*, Bingley, UK: Emerald Group Publishing Limited, 211–22.

Valaei, N., S. Rezaei, R. C. Ho, and F. Okumus (2019). Beyond structural equation modelling in tourism research: Fuzzy set/qualitative comparative analysis (fs/qca) and data envelopment analysis (deA). In S. Rezaei (ed.), *Quantitative Tourism Research in Asia*, Singapore: Springer, 297–309.

von Wright, Georg Henrik (1941/1965). *The Logical Problem of Induction*. 1941 original edition, 1965 2nd revised edition. Oxford: Basil Blackwell. Quotes are from the 1965 edition.

Weick, Karl E. (1995). *Sensemaking*. Thousand Oaks, CA: Sage.

Weick, K. E. (2011). Reflections: Change agents as change poets – On reconnecting flux and hunches. *Journal of Change Management*, 11(1): 7–20.

White, M., and D. Epston (1990). *Narrative Means to Therapeutic Ends*. New York, London: W.W. Norton and Company.

Wolfe, F. A. (1988). *Taking the Quantum Leap: The New Physics for Nonscientists*. New York: HarperPerennial.

Worley, C. G., V. Zardet, M. Bonnet, and A. Savall (2015). *Becoming Agile: How the SEAM Approach to Management Builds Adaptability*. Hoboken, NJ: John Wiley and Sons.

Žižek, S. (2012). *Less than Nothing: Hegel and the Shadow of Dialectical Materialism*. London, New York: Verso Books.

Index